NEW JERSEY PATRIOTS

Their Lives, Contributions, and Burial Sites

JOE FARRELL • LAWRENCE KNORR • JOE FARLEY

SUNBURY PRESS

Mechanicsburg, PA USA

Published by Sunbury Press, Inc.
Mechanicsburg, Pennsylvania

SUNBURY
P R E S S
www.sunburypress.com

For information about special discounts for bulk purchases, please contact Sunbury Press Orders Dept. at (855) 338-8359 or orders@sunburypress.com.

To request one of our authors for speaking engagements or book signings, please contact Sunbury Press Publicity Dept. at publicity@sunburypress.com.

FIRST SUNBURY PRESS EDITION: November 2024

Set in Adobe Garamond | Interior design by Crystal Devine | Cover by Lawrence Knorr | Edited by the authors.

Publisher's Cataloging-in-Publication Data
Names: Farrell, Joe, author | Farley, Joe, author | Knorr, Lawrence, author.
Title: New Jersey patriots : their lives, contributions, and burial sites / Joe Farrell Lawrence Knorr Joe Farley.
Description: First trade paperback edition. | Mechanicsburg, PA : Sunbury Press, 2024.
Summary: The individuals from New Jersey who played prominent roles in the founding of the USA are detailed.
Identifiers: ISBN 979-8-88819-243-6 (softcover).
Subjects: HISTORY / United States / Revolutionary Period (1775-1800) | BIOGRAPHY & AUTOBIOGRAPHY / Political.

Designed in the USA
0 1 1 2 3 5 8 13 21 34 55

For the Love of Books!

Contents

Introduction

When discussing the Revolutionary War patriots from New Jersey, the conversation is always tempered by the number of Loyalists, especially the situation with William Franklin, the last colonial governor of New Jersey, who was the son of Benjamin Franklin. William Franklin remained loyal to the crown to the end, much to the dismay of his father. William led the Loyalists in New York and New Jersey after he was incarcerated after the Declaration of Independence. Ultimately, he moved to England, where he spent the rest of his life.

Instead, we pick up the story of William Livingston, the first governor of New Jersey post-Declaration. During the early days, there were several attempts by Loyalists to kidnap Livingston, to no avail. He was both a military and political leader and guided the early formation of the colony's rebel government.

Two other prominent men from New Jersey could have received top billing rather than Livingston. William Alexander, also known as Lord Stirling, was an outright hero, referred to at the time as "The Bravest Man in America." Stirling risked his life during his military career, though he was probably too fond of drink.

Aaron Burr was always in the limelight, narrowly missing the chance to become one of our first presidents. Of course, he became infamous for his duel with the beloved Alexander Hamilton. He was also embroiled in a bizarre scheme concerning the West. Regardless of his reputation, Burr's life was very interesting, indeed.

Other notables include a President of Congress, Elias Boudinot, who was the leader of the Continental of Congress at the time of the Treaty of Paris; John Witherspoon, a clergyman and President of Princeton; and Stephen Crane, the great-grandfather of the famous novelist.

Many of the other New Jersey Founders were challenged by the colony being a crossroads of armies, the British in New York and the Patriots in Pennsylvania crossed paths many times early and later in the war. Some lost everything they owned to the cause, and quite a few of them also had connections in New York City.

While none of the New Jersey Founders ended up in the category of Washington, Adams, Jefferson, Madison, Jay, or Franklin, they all played important roles in shaping the formation of this important colony into our third state to adopt the Constitution after Delaware and Pennsylvania.

Lawrence Knorr

William Livingston
(1723–1790)

"First Governor of New Jersey"

Buried at Green-Wood Cemetery,
Brooklyn, New York.

Continental Association • Governor • Constitution

William Livingston is best known as the first Governor of New Jersey following the Declaration of Independence. He was the brother of Philip Livingston, who signed that document. Livingston also served in the Continental Congress, where he signed the Continental Association. He was a delegate to the Constitutional Convention and signed the US Constitution.

Livingston, born November 30, 1723, in Albany, New York, was a son of Philip Livingston (1686–1749), the 2nd Lord of Livingston Manor, and his wife, Catherine (née Van Brugh) Livingston, the only child of Pieter Van Brugh, the Mayor of Albany. Livingston's siblings included Robert Livingston (1708–1790), the 3rd Lord of Livingston Manor; Peter Van Brugh Livingston (1710–1792), the Treasurer of New York; and Philip Livingston (1716–1778), a future signer of the Declaration of Independence.

Livingston was educated by tutors and in the local schools. When he was 13, he lived among the Iroquois in the Mohawk Valley with Henry Barclay, an Anglican missionary and Yale graduate. Livingston then enrolled at Yale at age 14 in 1737 and graduated in 1741, having

William Livingston

studied multiple languages and writing. Following his father's wishes, he next studied law under James Alexander in New York City and became his clerk. Alexander was the father of William Alexander, who became known as Lord Stirling and was a prominent major general during the Revolution. Livingston soon found himself bored with his law studies, and in the spring of 1746, he wrote an anonymous article attacking his boss's wife, Mary Spratt Provoost Alexander, a successful merchant. Alexander terminated the apprenticeship.

During this time, the young Livingston continued his writing and, in 1747, penned the pastoral poem "Philosophic Solitude, or the Choice of a Rural Life." This was one of the first successful poems by an American and was published many times by the 1800s.

Not deterred, Livingston's father found legal work for his son with William Smith, Sr., another leading attorney. Livingston studied with William Smith, Jr., and was admitted to the New York bar in 1748. He then set up a practice in New York City and Albany.

Livingston married Susannah French, the daughter of Philip French III and Susanna (née Brockholst) French, in 1748. The couple had 13 children, seven of whom lived to adulthood. Livingston also developed business associations with William Alexander, Lord Stirling, and John Morin Scott, a future Continental Congressman.

In 1752, Livingston was appointed by the New York colonial legislature to publish a history of the statutes enacted since the colony's founding, entitled *Digest of the Laws of the Colony, 1691–1751*. With partners William Smith, Jr., and John Morin Scott, he started a weekly journal, the *Independent Reflector*, the first New York newspaper to be critical of Catholic and Anglican Church activities in the New York City area. The three owners, Presbyterians, were called "The Triumvirate" by their contemporaries, who met weekly at The King's Arms tavern in an association dubbed The Whig Club, drinking to the memories of Oliver Cromwell and John Hampden. Their activities may have prevented the installation of an Anglican bishop in New York and diminished investment in King's College, which ultimately became Columbia University, founded by Anglicans. This put them at odds with New York Chief Justice James De Lancey, James Alexander, and Reverend Henry Barclay, Livingston's tutor.

The *Independent Reflector* only lasted until late 1753, after which Livingston published independent essays in the *New York Mercury* under the heading "The Watch Tower." These were early writings opposing a state-sanctioned church. King's College opened on October 31, 1754, and never appointed a bishop.

In 1754, Livingston was a commissioner working on the boundaries between New York and Massachusetts. He also helped to found the New York Society Library, which is still in existence. He then served briefly in the New York Provincial Assembly from 1759 to 1761, representing Livingston Manor in a rotation of family members through the office. In 1764, Livingston was back at negotiating boundaries, this time between New Jersey and New York. He was elected to the American Philosophical Society in 1768.

Livingston was back to writing history in 1770, releasing a history of the French and Indian War from the British perspective. In 1772, at age 49, he retired to New Jersey, moving to his wife's home in Elizabethtown. That winter, a fifteen-year-old Alexander Hamilton stayed with them while attending Francis Barber's grammar school. Livingston purchased land in Elizabethtown and started construction of a mansion dubbed Liberty Hall. It was completed in 1773 and stands to this day.

As tensions mounted with England, in December 1773, Livingston was among the Elizabethtown Committee of Correspondence, including Stephen Crane, John De Hart, William P. Smith, Elias Boudinot, and John Chetwood. On July 23, 1774, the New York legislature appointed Livingston to the First Continental Congress. There, he signed the Continental Association. He was then appointed to the Second Continental Congress, serving until June 1776, before the signing of the Declaration of Independence. Rather, he returned to New Jersey, which had declared its statehood and appointed Livingston as its first governor.

Livingston remained the governor of New Jersey for the rest of his life. During the early years immediately following independence, with the British headquartered in New York City, New Jersey was in a precarious position. Livingston dealt with Loyalists attempting to trade with the British and the regular movements of British troops through its borders. Between 1776 and 1779, Livingston moved his family to the Bowers-Livingston-Osborn House in Parsippany to stay away from British sympathizers and to avoid capture. There was a significant bounty on Livington's head, and the British frequently visited and looted Liberty Hall in his absence.

In June 1777, Livingston helped start a newspaper called the *New Jersey Gazette* that would be loyal to the cause. He then contributed to it with polemics and articles written under fourteen different pseudonyms. Scholars have dubbed him one of the most important propagandists in the colonies and certainly in New Jersey.

In June 1779, Loyalists raided the Parsippany home based on false information that Livingston would be there. Fortunately, he was not, and the perpetrators were captured. It is surmised a distant relative, the Loyalist mayor of New York City, David Mathews, was behind the attempt. The Livingstons returned to Liberty Hall later in 1779 and began restoring the property. In 1782, Livingston was honored to be a fellow of the American Academy of the Arts and Sciences.

In 1787, Livingston was elected to attend the Constitutional Convention on behalf of New Jersey. At 63, as one of the older delegates, his health limited his participation, but he did support the New Jersey

Plan, which defended the representation of the smaller states. Livingston, along with David Brearly, William Paterson, and Jonathan Dayton, signed the Constitution on behalf of New Jersey. Livingston was asked, the following year, to be the Minister to the Netherlands, but he declined the position. He wrote a commentary (in French) comparing the government of England with the new US Constitution entitled *Examen du Gouvernement d'Angleterre comparé aux Constitutions des Etats-Unis*. At the outset of the French Revolution, Emmanuel-Joseph Sieyès cited Livingston's commentary in his pamphlet *What Is the Third Estate?*

The grave of William Livingston.

Susannah Livingston died in July 1789 and was initially buried in the Trinity Churchyard in lower Manhattan. Livingston "very much regretted" her passing, according to the local newspapers. Meanwhile, he oversaw the implementation of the new state and federal offices for New Jersey under the new US Constitution.

Livingston died in Elizabeth, New Jersey, on July 25, 1790. He was 66. Wrote the *Federal Gazette*, ". . . America bewails the loss of one of her most distinguished patriots . . ." Livingston was interred next to his wife at Trinity Churchyard in New York City. In 1844, both husband and wife were exhumed and moved to Green-Wood Cemetery in Brooklyn, New York.

William and Susannah's children included:

• Susannah Livingston (1748–1840) married John Cleves Symmes (1742–1814) and became the stepmother-in-law of President William Henry Harrison.
• Catherine Livingston (1751–1813) married Matthew Ridley (1746–1789) and later her cousin John Livingston (1750–1822), son of Robert Livingston.

- Mary Livingston (born 1753) married James Linn in May 1771.
- William Livingston Jr. (1754–1817) married Mary Lennington.
- Philip Van Brugh Livingston (born 1755) died unmarried.
- Sarah Livingston (1756–1802) was educated at home and raised to be politically aware, even serving as her father's secretary. At only 17, she married John Jay and accompanied him to Spain and Paris, where he helped negotiate the Treaty of Paris in 1783. Sarah is credited with writing the toast used to celebrate the treaty at the official dinner. Back in New York, Jay was appointed the Secretary of Foreign Affairs, and the couple established weekly diplomatic dinners in the new capital, New York City. She was also First Lady of New York when her husband was governor and then wife of the 1st Chief Justice of the Supreme Court.
- Henry Brockholst Livingston (1757–1823) was a lawyer who became a member of the US Supreme Court (1807–1823). He is buried in Green-Wood Cemetery.
- Judith Livingston (1758–1843) married John W. Watkins, an attorney.
- Philip French Livingston (1760–c. 1765) drowned in a boating accident in the Hackensack River.
- John Lawrence Livingston (1762–1781) died at sea aboard the USS *Saratoga*.

Other interesting descendants of William Livingston include:

- Julia Kean, the wife of Hamilton Fish, former Governor of New York and US Secretary of State.
- Thomas Kean, former Governor of New Jersey.
- Edwin Brockholst Livingston was a historian who focused on the Livingston family history.
- Henry Brockholst Ledyard, former Mayor of Detroit.

William Livingston is honored by the town of Livingston, New Jersey; Governor Livingston High School in Berkeley Heights, New Jersey; and the Livingston campus at Rutgers University.

William Alexander, Lord Stirling
(1725 – 1783)

"The Bravest Man in America"

Buried at Albany Rural Cemetery,
Menands, New York.

———————

Major General

William Alexander, also known as Lord Stirling, was a major general during the American Revolution who was a close friend of George Washington, ranking third or fourth in the chain of command in the Continental Army. Alexander was a wealthy man who often self-funded his military units. He was known for his courage on the battlefield and was dubbed "The Bravest Man in America" by a newspaper following his actions on Long Island. He was the general who unraveled the Conway Cabal. His claim to a Scottish earldom was dubious, but he used the title throughout his life.

———————

Alexander, born December 27, 1725, in New York, New York, was the son of James Alexander (1691–1756), the Attorney General of New York, and his wife, Mary (née Spratt Provoost) Alexander (1693–1760). The elder Alexander was a distant relative of Henry Alexander, the 5th Earl of Sterling, who died in 1739, but he never pursued the title. He had fled Scotland after the failed Jacobite uprising and had success in America, emigrating with his wife in 1716. Mother Mary was a successful merchant, descended from the Spratt and de Peyster families and the stepdaughter of David Provoost, a successful Huguenot merchant in New York. Mary took over the Provoost business and grew it to the point

William Alexander, Lord Stirling

where she was one of the largest merchants in New York City, especially during the time of the French and Indian War.

Young Alexander was educated privately, studying law under his father's direction, and demonstrated aptitudes in mathematics and astronomy. He assisted his mother in her import business. In 1748, Alexander married Sarah Livingston, the daughter of Philip Livingston, the 2nd Lord of Livingston Manor, and the sister of William Livingston, the Governor of New Jersey. The couple eventually had two daughters and one son: Mary Alexander (1749–1820), who married the merchant Robert Watts (1743–1814), the son of John Watts of New York; Catherine Alexander (1755–1826), who married Continental Congressman William Duer (1743–1799); and William Alexander, who died in infancy.

Alexander struck up a partnership with his brother-in-law, Hendrick "Henry" Livingston, who was based in Jamaica. They imported goods from England into the Hudson Valley, purchasing two ships for this purpose. William was also a captain in the local militia and routinely drilled his recruits.

In June 1754, Alexander attended the Albany Congress on behalf of his father, who was ill. There, he witnessed the presentation of Benjamin Franklin's Albany Plan of Union, the first plan to unify the colonies under a national government. He also met with representatives of the Iroquois Confederacy to discuss the Livingston family land claims in dispute. He offered lands back to the Iroquois that he would likely not accrue to him as part of his father-in-law's estate. Alexander also represented the Penns in their efforts to purchase more land for Pennsylvania.

After the conference, Massachusetts Governor William Shirley, who supported an attack on the French, asked Alexander to help him plan an attack on Fort Niagara, near present-day Buffalo, New York. Alexander procured provisions and boats and prepared for the attack. When William Johnson began planning an attack on the French at Lake George, the two began competing for the same resources, which led to disagreement. Neither attack was successful, and Shirley was replaced as the British military leader in North America.

In 1756, Alexander accompanied Shirley to England to testify on the latter's behalf as he defended his actions. Alexander ended up staying for nearly five years in England. While there, he learned of the vacant earldom in Scotland. At the encouragement of two Scottish lords, Archibald Campbell, the 3rd Duke of Argyll, and John Stuart, the 3rd Earl of Bute, Alexander pursued the Earldom of Stirling. The last earl had died in 1739, and the peerage was extinct unless filled. Alexander's sponsors believed Alexander stood to inherit vast lands in if approved, and they awaited their cut as a reward. The lands included large sections of Nantucket, Long Island, New Brunswick, Martha's Vineyard, Nova Scotia, and a large portion of what is now Maine. The Duke of York had purchased Long Island from the late earl's estate for 7,000 British pounds, but the sum had not been transferred due to the line dying out. While Alexander was descended from the 1st Earl of Stirling, he was a distant relation of the late 5th Earl. In 1759, a Scottish court in Edinburgh ruled unanimously in favor of the case, and Alexander adopted the title. However, against the advice of his sponsors, Alexander sought validation in the House of Lords as required by British law. They denied the claim, and though the lands were not acquired, Alexander kept using the title in America without their approval.

Regardless, Alexander returned to New York in 1761 on the same ship as his friend Philip Schuyler, having inherited a large fortune from his father, including mining and agricultural enterprises. Using the title Lord Stirling, he lived an extravagant lifestyle and built a grand estate in Basking Ridge, Bernards Township, New Jersey. Upon its completion, he moved there from New York City. When his mother passed away in 1763, he also inherited her fortune.

In New Jersey, Lord Stirling entertained often and lavishly. He was a member of the New Jersey Provincial Council and the Surveyor General. George Washington was a frequent guest, and he gave away Alexander's daughter at her wedding. Due to his successful attempts at winemaking in New Jersey, the Royal Society of Arts awarded Alexander a gold medal for winning the challenge of making wine in America. Alexander had planted 2100 grapevines on his estate. He was elected to the American Philosophical Society in 1770.

As tensions arose with England, Alexander sided with the Patriots, joining the New Jersey Council of Safety. He was expelled from the Royal Militia units he had been part of in New York and New Jersey.

In November 1775, he was appointed colonel of the 1st New Jersey Regiment of militia, which he funded himself. In January 1776, he led a group of volunteers to successfully capture a British transport ship in New York Bay.

In March 1776, Congress appointed Alexander as a brigadier general in the Continental Army upon the recommendation of Major General Charles Lee. He was initially in command at New York City where he supervised the fortifications of the city and harbor under the commander of the Northern Department, Philip Schuyler, based in Albany. He was then assigned to the 1st Maryland Regiment in Sullivan's division during the Battle of Long Island in August 1776. Alexander and his men faced repeated attacks and heavy losses from British General James Grant at the Old Stone House near Gowanus Creek. Realizing the British were overwhelming his forces; he implemented a rear-guard action that delayed the British attacks while the bulk of his troops escaped Brooklyn Heights. Alexander himself stayed behind to lead a counterattack, allowing Washington and his troops to eventually evacuate to Manhattan in the fog overnight. Said Washington at the time, "Good God! What brave fellows

I must this day lose." The fighting devolved to hand-to-hand combat, and only ten Americans survived. Two of the survivors, Generals Sullivan and Alexander, were captured by the British and spent several months as prisoners in New York City in the company of the Howe brothers. Both Washington and the British praised Alexander for his courage, audacity, and leadership. The British said he "fought like a wolf." An American newspaper described him as "the bravest man in America."

During their captivity, the Howes tried to turn the generals to the British to no avail, though some British officers quipped Alexander should be returned in order to preserve the supply of good wine. Alexander was returned in a prisoner exchange for Governor (of British West Florida) Montfort Browne and fought at the Battle of Trenton in December 1776, where he received the surrender of a Hessian regiment.

On February 19, 1777, Alexander was promoted to major general and initially served in the Hudson Highlands. For the balance of the Revolution, Alexander ranked third or fourth in the Continental Army, fighting at Metuchen, Brandywine, and Germantown.

During the bitter winter of 1777/78, the Continental Army was at Valley Forge. The British had occupied Philadelphia, and the Congress was in York, Pennsylvania. At this time, a young major named James Monroe was Alexander's aide-de-camp stationed at his headquarters. In later years, Aaron Burr criticized Monroe, saying his duty was to refill Alexander's tankard and listen to his stories about himself. Also during this time, General Horatio Gates was whispered as a possible replacement for George Washington. While one of Gates's aides, James Wilkinson, was at Alexander's headquarters in Tredyffrin Township, Chester County, Pennsylvania, he got drunk over dinner and began berating Washington, sharing criticisms from other officers. He revealed to Alexander he had read a letter from Thomas Conway to Gates urging him to "save the country." Alexander wrote to Washington (and other members of Congress) the next day, sharing what Wilkinson had said. Washington then confronted Conway, who called Alexander a liar and denied the note's existence. However, Gates made statements that betrayed his guilt. The Conway Cabal then unraveled.

On June 12, 1778, while at the Continental Congress in York, brother-in-law and Declaration of Independence signer Philip Livingston died. Alexander was away in New Jersey. On June 28, 1778, at the Battle of Monmouth, he led the Left Wing of the Army, holding off a critical British flanking maneuver. Then, from July 4 to August 12, Alexander presided over the court martial of Major General Charles Lee. Lee, the 2nd in command at Monmouth, had disobeyed Washington's orders to attack. Lee was found guilty and suspended from command.

From December 21, 1778, until February 5, 1779, while George Washington was with Congress in Philadelphia, he put Alexander in charge of the Army while encamped at Middlebrook, New Jersey, headquartered at the Van Horne House.

In August 1779, with "Lighthorse Harry" Lee, Alexander supported a successful raid on Paulus Hook, now Jersey City, New Jersey. He then managed the Staten Island expedition of January 14 to 15, 1780. Later that year, he sat on the board of inquiry regarding the actions of British spy Major John André. This exposed Benedict Arnold's treachery and led to André's execution by hanging on October 2, 1780.

As the focus of the war shifted South to Yorktown, Washington awarded Alexander command of the Northern Department, headquartered in Albany, New York, in October 1781. There, he countered a British attack from Lake George that fizzled after the Yorktown surrender.

During the interim period from the victory in Virginia at Yorktown until the Treaty of Paris, Alexander was stationed in Albany. There, he continued his lavish eating and drinking, leading to severe gout and rheumatism. By November 1782, his health had deteriorated rapidly. He was losing the use of his hands. By December, he was fervid and bedridden. His wife and daughter cared for him. Major General William Alexander died at Albany on January 15, 1783.

Alexander was initially buried at Trinity Churchyard in New York City. A memorial tablet to the Alexander family there faces the historic Wall Street district adjoining St. Paul's Chapel.

Eventually, Alexander was reinterred at Albany Rural Cemetery in Menands, New York, in the Church Grounds, Section 49, Lot 12.

Ninety years after the Battle of Brooklyn, a commemorative monument was erected to honor the brave men who fought and died there in the Revolution. While excavating the monument, known as Prospect Park, the bones of many soldiers were discovered. This hallowed ground

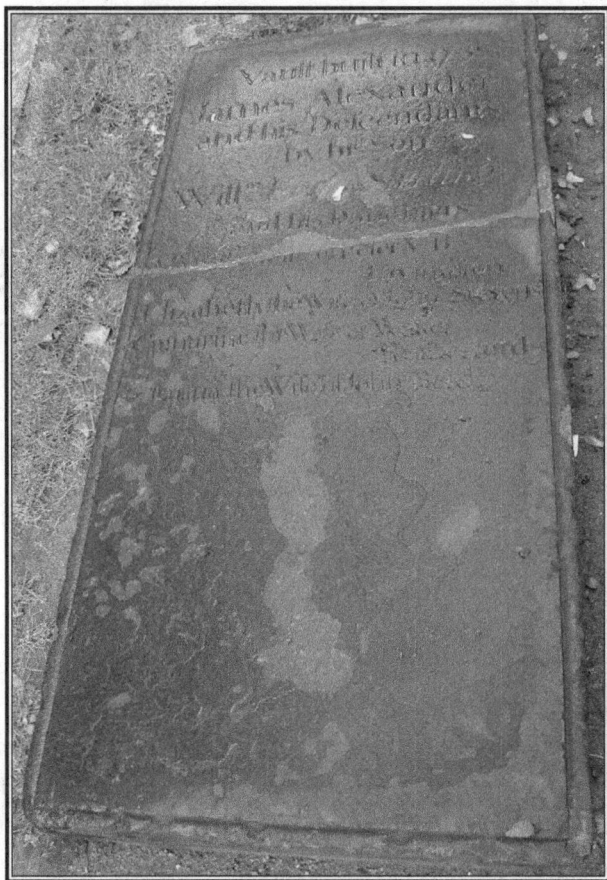

The grave of William Alexander.

in New York was deeded to the State of Maryland in honor of the blood-soaked ground on which their soldiers had fallen.

William Alexander, Lord Stirling, is honored in many ways, including schools and parks in New Jersey. The town of Sterling, Massachusetts, and Sterling Place in Brooklyn, New York, are named after him.

Through his daughter Catherine, his descendants include Columbia University president William Alexander Duer, lawyer and jurist John Duer, U.S. Congressman William Duer, and writer and suffragette Alice Duer Miller.

Through his daughter Mary, his descendants include General Stephen Watts Kearny and General Philip Kearny, Jr., who was killed in action during the Civil War.

Elias Boudinot
(1740 – 1821)

President During the Treaty of Paris

Buried at Saint Mary's Episcopal Churchyard,
Burlington, New Jersey.

———————

Military • US Congress • Mint Director

Elias Boudinot was a deeply devout Christian, abolitionist, lawyer, states-
man, and soldier who served under George Washington as an intelligence
officer and commissary for prisoners of war. Boudinot served in the
Continental Congress and was its president at the end of the Revolution.
He later served as a member of the US House of Representatives and as
the Director of the US Mint. In 1816, he founded the American Bible
Society which has since distributed billions of Bibles worldwide. As a
Congressman, he proposed a national day of Thanksgiving.

———————

Boudinot was born on May 2, 1740, in Philadelphia, Pennsylvania, to
Elias Boudinot III and his wife, Mary Catherine (née Williams) Boudinot.
The elder Boudinot was a merchant and silversmith who was a neighbor
and friend of Benjamin Franklin. Boudinot's paternal lineage was French
Huguenot. His mother's ancestors were Welsh. The couple married in
1729 and had nine children, five of whom reached adulthood. Sister
Annis became the first published female poet in the colonies. Brother
Elisha later became Chief Justice of the New Jersey Supreme Court.

Boudinot was tutored in the classics at home and then studied law
under Richard Stockton in Princeton, New Jersey, who had married his

Elias Boudinot

sister Annis. In 1760, Boudinot was admitted to the New Jersey bar and set up a prosperous law practice in Elizabeth, New Jersey. On April 21, 1762, he married Hannah Stockton, his brother-in-law's younger sister. The Boudinots had nine children, four of whom survived to adulthood. One daughter, Susan, later married William Bradford, who became the Chief Justice of Pennsylvania and US Attorney General in the Washington administration.

Boudinot largely avoided politics prior to the Revolution. In 1774, he joined the Essex County Committee of Correspondence and chaired the county's Committee of Safety. He was also elected to the Provincial Congress of New Jersey in 1775. During these early months, Boudinot held out for reconciliation with England, even after the first shots were fired at Lexington and Concord. At a meeting in New Brunswick in April 1776, he voted against Dr. John Witherspoon's call for New Jersey's independence, though he hoped the Continental Congress would address the matter. Wrote Boudinot later:

There appeared a general Approbation of the Measure, and I strongly suspected a universal Acquiescence of both Committees & Audience in approving the doctor's scheme . . . I never felt myself in a more mortifying Situation . . . Two of the Committee had delayed the Question by speaking in favor of it, but no one had spoken in Opposition, till I arose and in a Speech of about half an Hour or better, stated my peculiar Situation and endeavored to show the Fallacy of the Doctor's Arguments.

As Congress declared independence, with his brother-in-law's signature, Boudinot assisted the Patriot cause. He promoted enlistments, loaned money for supplies, and was the aide-decamp to William Livingston of the New Jersey militia. He was also involved in spy activities monitoring the British during the occupation of New York City from Staten Island and Long Island.

Impressed with Boudinot's work with Livingston, George Washington appointed him the Commissary General for Prisoners on May 5, 1777. Congress's Board of War agreed, and Boudinot was commissioned as a colonel in the Continental Army, serving until July 1778. In this role, he was responsible for supplying the American prisoners held by the British. Boudinot was soon at odds with the Congress, who were unreasonable regarding prisoner exchanges with the British. Where General Howe had suggested simple officer for officer, soldier for soldier, citizen for citizen exchanges, the Congress demanded hard currency. This made Boudinot's job more difficult and risked the treatment of prisoners. On March 8, 1778, he was summoned to Philadelphia for a meeting with an oversight committee of Congress where he explained his position for the fair treatment of prisoners on both sides as both moral and ethical and reflective of the wishes of General Washington. Boudinot, who had been elected to the Congress months earlier and had not taken his seat, filed his report. He had used his own money to fund the supplies for the prisoners. Wrote Boudinot at the time:

When I found every application to obtain hard money from Congress for the Cloathing of our Prisoners in vain, I waited on Genl Washington, and proposed my resignation, as my Character was at stake, having (on the promise of the Secret Committee to yield me every necessary aid) pledged myself to the officers in Confinement that they should be regularly supplied with every necessary, but they now suffered more than ever. In much distress and with Tears in his Eyes, he assured me that if he was deserted by the Gentn of the Country, he should despair. He could not do everything . . . He was Gen. Quarter Master and Commissary. Everything fell on him and he was unequal to the task. He gave me the most positive Engagement that if I would contrive any mode for their Support and Comfort he would confirm it as far as was in his Power—On this I told him, I knew of but one way and that was to borrow Money on my own private Security. He assured me that in Case I did, and was not reimbursed by Congress, he would go an equal share with me in the loss. I then formed the plan of obliging Genl. Burgoyne to pay hard money for the support of the British Prisoners whom we supplied with daily rations, and in the meantime proceeded to borrow money or take Goods in New York on my own Credit. Thus I furnished 300 officers with a handsome suit of Cloaths each, and 1100 Men with a plain suit, Found them Blanketts, Shirts etc. and added to their provisions found by the British a full half ration of Bread and Beef p[e]r. day for upwards of 15 Months. Part of this I supplied by sending wheat and flour to New York, and selling them for hard money, under leave from Genl Robertson. Sometime in the beginning of the year 1778, Congress recd from Genl Burgoyne nearly 40,000 Dollars in hard money. In the beginning of 1778, I was chosen a Member of Congress, but continued in the Army till June, when Genl. Washington, knowing that I was near thirty Thousand Dollars in advance for the Prisoners, urged me to go and take my Seat in Congress, where I might get some of the hard money recd from Genl[.] Burgoyne before it was all expended, for if it was once gone, I should be totally ruined. I accordingly left the Army and joined Congress on their return from York Town in Pennsylvania, after the British had evacuated the City of Philadelphia. [10]

In July, he resigned from the commissary role, as General Washington suggested, and took his seat in Congress as a delegate from New Jersey.

In this new role, he continued to advocate for the treatment of prisoners. Boudinot left the Congress in 1779. But was reelected in 1781 and served through 1784. He was involved in the debates over the Articles of Confederation and the peace treaty with Britain. On November 4, 1782, despite his difficulties in the past with the Congress over prisoners, Boudinot was elected the President of the Confederation Congress, succeeding John Hanson. During Boudinot's year in the role, he signed the peace treaty with Great Britain on April 15, 1783. In June 1783, he led Congress's move from Philadelphia to Princeton, where they met at Nassau Hall on the college campus.

Boudinot left Congress at the end of his term and returned to New Jersey to practice law. After the US Constitution was ratified, he ran for office in the House of Representatives and served in the First through Third Congresses (from 1789 to 1795). On September 25, 1789, the day after the House of Representatives voted to recommend the First Amendment of the newly drafted Constitution to the states for ratification, Congressman Boudinot proposed that the House and Senate jointly request President Washington to proclaim a day of thanksgiving for "the many signal favors of Almighty God." Said Boudinot:

> "I cannot think of letting the session pass over without offering an opportunity to all the citizens of the United States of joining, with one voice, in returning to Almighty God their sincere thanks for the many blessings he had poured down upon them."

President Washington officially declared the Thanksgiving Holiday on October 3, 1789, setting the first official date as November 26, 1789.

Boudinot refused to align with political parties and was one of only nine representatives who voted against the Eleventh Amendment of the Constitution, regarding jurisdictional standing in lawsuits.

Following the death of his son-in-law, William Bradford, in 1795, daughter Susan, now a widow, moved in with her parents and began editing her father's papers regarding the Revolutionary era. In October of that year, President Washington named Boudinot to succeed David Rittenhouse as the Director of the US Mint in Philadelphia. He kept this position until resigning in July 1805. When he, Hannah, and Susan moved to a new home in Burlington, New Jersey. Hannah died a few years after the move, leaving Boudinot a widower with his daughter.

In addition to numerous civic, religious, and educational causes, for nearly fifty years, Boudinot was a trustee for Princeton University. He also speculated on large tracts of land in Ohio, owning more of Green Township in what is now the western suburbs of Cincinnati. In response to Thomas Paine's deistic *The Age of Reason* (1794), Boudinot wrote, in 1801, the Christian response, *The Age of Revelation*. He was elected as a member of the American Antiquarian Society in 1814. In 1816, a devout Presbyterian, he founded the American Bible Society and served as its president for the rest of his life.

The grave of Elias Boudinot.

David Brearley
(1745 – 1790)

Judge and Master Mason

Buried at Saint Michael's Church Cemetery,
Trenton, New Jersey.

Signer of the US Constitution • Military

David Brearley was the Chief Justice of the New Jersey Supreme Court, a delegate from New Jersey to the Constitutional Convention, a signer of the US Constitution, and a US District Court Judge for New Jersey.

Brearley was born on June 11, 1745, at Spring Grove Farm, in Lawrence Township, Mercer County, New Jersey, to David Brearley Sr. and his wife, Mary.

Brearley attended Princeton University, then the College of New Jersey, but did not graduate. He read law and entered private practice at Allentown, New Jersey through 1775. Circa 1767, Brearley married Elizabeth Mullen.

Upon the outbreak of the war, in late 1775, Brearley's brother, Joseph, was commissioned a captain in the Second New Jersey Continental Regiment and saw service in Canada. Brearley agitated for independence and participated in the creation of a new constitution for independent New Jersey. In June 1776, he joined Colonel Philip Van Cortland's regiment as a lieutenant colonel. Brearley served for five months, fighting in and around New York, and then joined the retreat through New Jersey, when his term expired on November 30. He returned home to his wife in

David Brearley

Allentown, New Jersey, the next day. Brother Joseph soon arrived home, too, and decided to leave the Continental Army and serve locally with the First Hunterdon County Militia.

Brearley had been made a lieutenant colonel in the Fourth New Jersey Continental Regiment but switched to the First New Jersey Regiment on January 1, 1777. He fought in New Jersey against the British and Hessians who were trying to occupy the colony. He then served through the Philadelphia Campaign of 1777, at the Battles of Brandywine and Germantown. During this year, his wife, Elizabeth died. After winter at Valley Forge, he fought at the Battle of Monmouth in June 1778.

In March 1780. Brearley resigned from the military to become the Chief Justice of the New Jersey Supreme Court, serving until 1789. He wrote the decision for *Holmes v. Walton*, deciding that the judiciary had the authority to determine the constitutionality of laws. Princeton granted him an honorary M.A. degree afterward. In 1783, he married Elizabeth Higbee.

Brearley was elected a delegate from New Jersey to the Constitutional Convention of 1787. He was a close follower of William Paterson and his New Jersey Plan. He was the Chairman of the Committee of Postponed Parts, which provided many of the final edits of the document, including the presidency, vice presidency, Electoral College, method of impeachment, patents and copyrights, the role of the House of Representatives

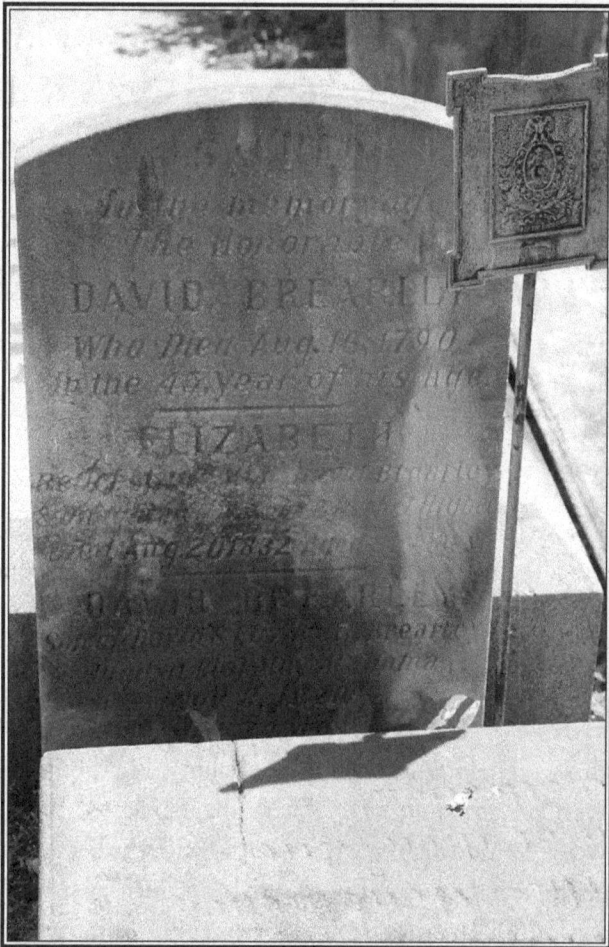

The grave of David Brearley.

regarding finance, Native American relations, and other matters. Brearley signed the US Constitution.

Brearley presided over the New Jersey convention to adopt the Constitution. Afterward, he was a presidential elector for George Washington. On September 25, 1789, President George Washington nominated Brearley to the US District Court for the District of New Jersey. He was confirmed by the Senate that day and received his commission the following day.

Besides his judicial duties, Brearley was the Grand Master of the Masonic Order in New Jersey and helped found, in 1783, the Society of the Cincinnati in the State of New Jersey. He was that order's vice president for the rest of his life. He also served as a delegate to the Episcopal General Conference of 1786 and helped to write their prayer book. In 1789, he was elected to the American Philosophical Society.

Only 45, Brearley suffered from a long illness that took him on August 16, 1790, in Trenton, New Jersey. He was interred in the churchyard at Saint Michael's Episcopal Church in Trenton, where a cenotaph was erected in 1924 in his honor. It reads:

> Sacred to the memory of the Hon. David Brearley, Lieutenant Colonel in the Army of the United States, a member of the state and federal conventions, nine years Chief Justice of New Jersey. As a soldier, he was cool, determined and brave; as a judge, intelligent and upright; as a citizen, an early, decided, and faithful patriot; in private and social life, irreproachable. He died, much regretted, 16th of August 1790, in the 45th year of his age.

Brearley Lodge Number 2 in Bridgeton, New Jersey is a Masonic Lodge named in his honor. Several streets in Wisconsin and New Jersey are named for him, as is David Brearley High School in Kenilworth, New Jersey.

Aaron Burr
(1756–1836)

Rival of Hamilton

Buried at Princeton Cemetery,
Princeton, New Jersey.

———•◦•———

Military • Third Vice President

He is said to be one of the most brilliant students to graduate from Princeton in the 18th century. He served his country with distinction during the American Revolution. He was instrumental and perhaps the man most responsible for Thomas Jefferson's election to the office of President of the United States. He served as Vice President during Jefferson's first term but is most remembered for killing the former Secretary of the Treasury Alexander Hamilton in America's most famous duel. He is the only Founder who was ever tried for treason and one of his biographers, Nancy Isenberg, titled her work *Fallen Founder*. Of all the Founders he could easily be singled out as the most historically maligned and misunderstood. He was born on February 6, 1756, in Newark, New Jersey and named Aaron Burr.

Burr's father the Reverend Aaron Burr was pastor of the First Presbyterian Church of Newark. He was also the second President of the College of New Jersey now known as Princeton. His mother, Esther Edwards Burr, was the daughter of Jonathan Edwards a famous minister noted for his beliefs in the teachings of John Calvin. Burr's father taught mathematics and ancient languages in addition to raising funds for the college. Before Burr reached his second birthday his very successful father caught a fever and passed away in 1757. Shortly after, Burr's mother died

Portrait of Aaron Burr, 1802, by John Vanderlyn.

after coming down with smallpox. Burr and his orphaned sister Sally were sent to Elizabethtown to live with their uncle Timothy Edwards who was a strict Puritan.

Burr didn't get along well with his uncle and tried to run away several times. At just eleven years of age, Burr presented himself as a prospective student to the college where his father had served as president. By all accounts, he was not even permitted to take the entrance exam that his father had created years before. He was rejected on the basis of being too young and too small. Two years later he was accepted at Princeton and graduated in 1772 at the age of eighteen. After briefly studying for the ministry, Burr decided that life was not for him and he traveled to Connecticut where he studied law at a school that had been established by his brother-in-law Tapping Reeve.

When the Revolution began, Burr was quick to join the American cause. Congress approved an assault on Canada where troops led by

Colonel Benedict Arnold would join forces led by Brigadier General Richard Montgomery in an attack on Quebec. Burr joined and served under Arnold's command on an arduous 600-mile march over unforgiving terrain to Quebec. He performed so well on this difficult journey that when Arnold and Montgomery joined forces, Burr was made a captain on the headquarters staff.

The actual assault of Quebec was led by Montgomery and Burr marched beside him. Grapeshot mortally wounded Montgomery who died in Burr's arms. Burr's attempts to rally the men behind him to continue the attack were countermanded by Montgomery's second in command. Montgomery's forces retreated and Arnold's were also overwhelmed. The assault on Quebec ended in failure but Burr's courage in the face of fire earned him the admiration of all those around him. A story, there is no way of knowing whether it is true, spread that as the retreat began the five-foot-six-inch Burr hoisted the body of his much larger commander on his shoulders and tried to retreat through deep snow before having to abandon his burden to avoid capture.

Upon his return home, with his fame having preceded him, Burr was offered and accepted a position on George Washington's staff. At the time Washington was preparing the defense of the city of New York. The two did not mesh. Though Burr was young, he was well-educated and had studied military tactics. He viewed Washington as an inexperienced Indian fighter who had yet to win a battle. Burr was quickly transferred as an aide to General Israel Putman where he received high marks for his valor and sound judgment.

Burr and Washington also clashed at the Battle of Monmouth fought in June 1778 in New Jersey. At one point Washington refused to allow Burr to lead an attack on a British position that Burr felt could have been easily taken. The battle itself was fought in intense summer heat and Burr suffered sunstroke. Burr requested and was granted a short leave of absence but his health failed to improve as quickly as he had hoped. On March 10, 1779, Washington accepted Colonel Burr's resignation with regrets. He retired with solid credentials as a hero of the Revolution.

In April of 1782, Burr set up a law practice in Albany. That same year he married the widow of a formal colonel in the British army, Theodosia Prevost. At age 36, Burr's new wife was ten years his senior and already the mother of five. Despite their age difference, the couple was happily married. One year later, she bore Burr a daughter who was named after her mother. Burr was totally devoted and attentive to both Theodosias. As a husband and father, even his worst enemies could find little in the way of criticism relative to his behavior.

Once peace with England was achieved, Burr moved his family back to New York and it was here his political career began. Within six months of his arrival, he was elected to the State Assembly. After serving his term during which he supported the abolition of slavery in New York, he returned to the practice of law. His knowledge and ability soon made him one of the leaders of the state bar. Another hero of the Revolution by the name of Alexander Hamilton was also a rising star in New York's legal circles. Though they disagreed fundamentally when it came to politics, both Burr and Hamilton respected each other during these years.

In 1789, Burr was appointed to the office of Attorney General for the State of New York by Governor Clinton. In 1791, with the support of two politically powerful New York families, the Clintons and the Livingstons, Burr was elected to the United States Senate defeating Hamilton's father-in-law Philip Schuyler. One of the reasons the Clintons and Livingstons backed Burr over Schuyler was the fact that in their view Hamilton had used his influence in the Washington administration to deny public offices to both families. Still, Hamilton did not direct his venom at those most responsible for the Schuyler defeat. Instead, he zeroed in on Burr. In the words of one of Burr's biographers, Milton Lomask, from this point on Hamilton's letters "would be filled with excoriations of Burr, with those flashes of naked hatred . . ."

In 1794, Burr's wife died after suffering a prolonged illness. Burr had come close to resigning his Senate seat in order to be with her in her last days. One of the things that may have stopped him was a letter he received from his eleven-year-old daughter who informed Burr that his wife was begging him not to leave Congress.

In the Presidential election of 1796, Burr received thirty electoral votes. When his Senate term ended, he returned to New York to restart his legal practice. He also busied himself strengthening New York's Republican party in preparation for the election of 1800. During the

election, Burr once again outmaneu-
vered Hamilton and New York's electoral votes were instrumental in giving
Thomas Jefferson the votes needed to
capture the presidency. As it turned
out, the Republicans nationwide were
loyal to their candidates as Jefferson
and Burr both received 73 electoral
votes which threw the election to
the House of Representatives. After
thirty-six ballots, the House elected
Jefferson and Burr was elected Vice
President. Almost immediately, Burr
was charged by various newspapers
and pamphleteers with having plotted
with Federalists to try to steal the presidency from Jefferson. This was highly
unlikely as in fact had Burr desired to

The grave of Aaron Burr at Princeton
Cemetery, Princeton, New Jersey
(photo by Lawrence Knorr).

make a deal with the opposition party he probably could have done so
easily as many Federalists preferred him to Jefferson. Still, the charges,
which may have been inspired by Hamilton, drove a wedge between
Jefferson and his Vice President.

By 1804 Jefferson had decided to remove Burr as his running mate.
As a result, Burr ran for the office of Governor of New York. He was
defeated in a bitterly contested race and ultimately came to blame scan-
dalous attacks on his character by Federalists in general and Hamilton
specifically for the loss. Burr wrote Hamilton a letter demanding a retrac-
tion of the charges that had been made against his character. The two
exchanged correspondence but the matter was not settled peacefully. On
July 11, 1804, Burr killed Hamilton in a duel. That meeting, perhaps the
most famous duel in history, effectively ended Burr's political life as well
as Hamilton's earthly existence.

After the duel, Burr returned to Washington to finish his term as
Vice President. By all accounts, he handled these duties admirably.
One of his final acts was presiding over the Senate impeachment trial

Detail of Burr's tombstone (photo by Lawrence Knorr).

of Supreme Court Justice Samuel Chase. It was no secret that Jefferson wanted Chase, a Federalist, removed from office. Burr was praised for the fair manner in which he conducted the trial. As a matter of fact, his conduct presiding over the trial drew praise from even those who had been critical of him. He was described as performing his duties "with the dignity and impartiality of an angel, but with the rigor of a devil." Chase was acquitted on all counts. Historians point to this case as the one that established the independence of the American judiciary.

In 1807, Jefferson had Burr arrested and tried on charges of conspiracy to lead an attack on territory under Spanish control and trying to separate those territories from the United States. He was acquitted of all charges. After the trial, Burr traveled to Europe where he lived for years before returning to America where he died at the age of eighty in 1836.

Perhaps it is time for Americans to judge Burr on his service to his country during the Revolution and in public office rather than on his duel with Hamilton. In fact we may want to remember him for his farewell remarks to the Senate as Vice President when he said that the Senate was a "sanctuary; a citadel of law, of order, and of liberty . . . and if the Constitution be destined ever to perish by the sacrilegious hands of the demagogue or the usurper, which God avert, its expiring agonies will be witnessed on this floor." After Burr left the room one of the senators who heard the speech reported that there was solemn and silent weeping for a full five minutes after Burr's exit.

Abraham Clark
(1726 – 1794)

House burned, sons tortured

Buried at Rahway Cemetery,
Rahway, New Jersey.

<hr>

**Continental Congress • Declaration of Independence
United States House of Representatives**

Abraham Clark suffered much for the independence of the United States. He served in the Continental Congress as a representative from New Jersey, voted for independence, and signed the Declaration of Independence. This, of course, was an act of treason and all the signers risked their lives and welfare. Many lost their homes and land, and property and many families were split up during the war.

<hr>

Abraham Clark was born in Elizabethtown (now Elizabeth), New Jersey, on February 15, 1726, the only child of Thomas Clark and Hannah Winans. At a young age, he established himself as a math prodigy. He was tutored in surveying, which gave him a steady income that allowed him to pursue an education in law. He was admitted to the state bar and quickly gained the reputation as a man for the little man as he would represent many who could not afford a lawyer. He became known as the "Poor Man's Counselor," was known for his integrity and generosity, and was very popular, particularly among the middle class.

Clark met Sarah Hatfield at the age of 22, and the couple was soon married. They had ten children, eight of whom survived to adulthood.

Abraham Clark (1726–1794)

Abraham Clark

He entered politics in 1752 when he served as clerk of the New Jersey colonial legislature. He later became Sheriff of Essex County and, in 1775, was elected to the Provincial Congress. The Provincial Congress was a transitional governing body of the province of New Jersey with representatives from all New Jersey's then thirteen counties to supersede the Royal Governor.

As the issue of independence heated up, Clark was highly vocal in favor of independence. Early in 1776, the New Jersey delegation to the Continental Congress was opposed to independence. On June 21, 1776, the state replaced all five delegates with delegates favoring separation, including Clark, John Hart, Francis Hopkinson, Richard Stockton, and John Witherspoon. They arrived in Philadelphia on June 28, 1776 and voted for the Declaration of Independence. On August 2, he signed the famous document. Few of the signers suffered as much as he did. The British invaded and burned his home and captured and tortured his sons.

Clark had two sons who were officers in the Continental Army. Aaron and Thomas were both officers in the New Jersey state artillery in Henry Knox's Regiment. Both were captured by the British and incarcerated on the prison ship *Jersey*, notorious for its brutality. Records said when the British discovered who they were, they were tortured and beaten. Thomas, for some reason, was put in the dungeon where he lay in his own urine, feces, and blood, and the only food he received was that pressed through a keyhole by fellow prisoners. Thomas most likely crossed the Delaware with George Washington, but in any event, he fought at the Battles of Trenton and Princeton and later at Brandywine, Germantown, and Monmouth. Abraham Clark never spoke of his sons' service and plight. He did not want them targeted by the enemy, nor did he seek special treatment for his sons. Now that Clark became aware of his sons' situation, he broke down and raised the issue in Congress. The British offered Abraham Clark the lives of his sons if he would recant the signing and support of the Declaration of Independence. He refused. When other members of Congress heard of the plight of Abraham's son, they were outraged. They ordered George Washington to take a British officer as a prisoner and starve him to death in a dark hole. The communication of that congressional order to General Howe was enough to end the persecution of Thomas, and he survived his imprisonment. He survived, but this cruel treatment permanently ruined his health, and he died at the age of thirty-five on May 13, 1789.

Clark knew what the signers were getting themselves into, and soon after the signing wrote to his friend, Colonel Elias Drayton: "as to my title, I know not yet whether it will be honorable or dishonorable; the issue of the war must settle it. Perhaps our Congress will be exalted on a high gallows . . . I assure you, Sir, I see, I feel, the danger we are in."

Clark remained in the Continental Congress until April 1778, when he was elected to the New Jersey Legislative Council. He was subsequently re-elected to Congress in 1780 until 1783, and then again from 1786 to 1788. He was one of New Jersey's representatives at the Annapolis Convention of 1786, at which representatives of five of the thirteen states gathered to address grievances that had arisen over the cumbersome Articles of Confederation. Among those attending were Alexander Hamilton, John Dickinson, Edmund Randolph, and James Madison.

Abraham Clark memorial.

Clark was elected to the Constitutional Convention of 1787 but was too ill to attend. The Constitution established a U.S. House of Representatives and a U.S. Senate and a plan for national elections. In 1790, Clark was elected to a seat in the House, serving in the Second (1791–93) and Third (1793–95) Congresses. He remained in Congress until his death. On September 15, 1794, Clark watched some men build a bridge on his land in what is now Roselle, New Jersey when he suddenly felt ill. Believing that he had suffered a bout of severe sunstroke, he staggered to his carriage and got himself home. There he was put to bed and died hours later. He was sixty-eight. He was buried in Rahway Cemetery next to his father. His wife survived him by a decade, and when she died, she was laid to rest with her husband. These words are inscribed on his tombstone: "he loved his country and adhered to her cause, in the darkest hours of her struggles against oppression."

On July 4, 1848, the citizens of Rahway erected a ten-foot obelisk monument in Clark's honor near his burial site. In 1924 the stone slabs marking both Abraham and Sarah's burial site were encased in a concrete monument. In 1941 a replica of Clark's original house was built about a block away from his original house. The original was destroyed in a fire in 1900. The replica is located at 101 West Ninth Avenue, Roselle, New Jersey. Visitation is by appointment. Abraham Clark High school stands just a few blocks from the home.

Clark is also memorialized in Washington, DC, in a large mural in the rotunda of the National Archives and John Trumbull's famous painting in the U.S. Capitol building.

George Clymer
(1739 – 1813)

A Pennsylvania Patriot

Buried at Friends' Burying Ground,
Trenton, New Jersey.

———•••———

Declaration of Independence • U.S. Constitution

George Clymer of Pennsylvania was an early proponent of independence from Great Britain. He was one of only five people who signed
both the Declaration of Independence and the Constitution. He was a
Continental Congressman and a member of the First Congress of the
United States in 1789.

———◆◆◆———

Clymer was born in Philadelphia on March 16, 1739, to Christopher
Clymer and Deborah (née Fitzwater) Clymer. Christopher was a ship's
captain who had emigrated from Bristol, England. He was the son of
Richard Clymer of Bristol. Deborah's parents were George Fitzwater and
Mary Hardiman, Quakers from Philadelphia. Christopher Clymer died
in 1740. Deborah followed a few years later or possibly remarried leaving
George an orphan at an early age.

Orphaned George was sent to live with his mother's sister and her husband, Hannah and William Coleman. Coleman was a wealthy merchant
who was a leader among the Quakers, also known as the Society of Friends.
Coleman saw to Clymer's education and George followed in Coleman's
footsteps as a merchant. In his 20s, Clymer worked in Coleman's count-
ing house and with Reese Meredith in 1764. Soon Meredith and Clymer

Portrait of George Clymer by Charles Willson Peale.

became business partners. Clymer married Reese Meredith's daughter Elizabeth in 1765, further cementing the business arrangements. The couple had nine children, five of whom lived to adulthood.

George Clymer joined the patriot cause around the time of the Sugar Act (1764) and the Stamp Act (1765). As a leader in the Philadelphia business community, he signed the nonimportation agreement that stymied trade with Britain and led to the repeal of the Stamp Act in 1766.

William Coleman died in 1769, leaving a large inheritance to Clymer. At the age of 39, Clymer was now independently wealthy and entered the political realm. He was elected to Philadelphia's City Council and was later a justice and an alderman. Following the British response to the Boston Tea Party in 1774, Clymer joined Pennsylvania's Committee of Correspondence calling for a meeting in Philadelphia that would become the First Continental Congress. He was named to the Congress and became the Continental Treasurer in July 1775, sharing the duties with Michael Hillegas. In November 1775, Clymer was appointed to the Pennsylvania Committee of Safety which took control of the government of Pennsylvania and saw to its defense.

Some of the initial delegates from Pennsylvania who were asked to sign the Declaration of Independence refused to do so, including John Dickinson, Andrew Allen, Charles Humphreys, and Thomas Willing. On July 20, 1776, Clymer, along with George Ross, Benjamin Rush, George Taylor, and James Wilson, were all elected to the Continental Congress with the express purpose of signing the Declaration. They did so, and though Clymer was late to sign it, "[he] affixed his signature to the manifesto, as if in the performance of an act which was about to consummate his dearest wishes, and realize those fond prospects of national prosperity which had ever been transcendent in his thoughts."

Clymer continued in his service as a Continental Congressman, visiting the army at Ticonderoga in September of 1776, and participating through 1777 and then 1780–1782. During this time, he also was a delegate to Pennsylvania's Constitutional Convention and helped form the Bank of Pennsylvania with Robert Morris. Morris and Clymer were then co-directors of the Bank of North America starting in 1781.

In 1787, Clymer, along with Ben Franklin and James Wilson, was named as Pennsylvania delegates to the Constitutional Convention. George was focused on the financial aspects of the proceedings including the assumption of war debts by the central government. Clymer was a strong proponent for a bicameral legislature. Upon ratification, Clymer was elected to the First Congress (1789–1791) but did not seek a second term.

Back in Pennsylvania, Clymer was the head of the Pennsylvania Department of Excise Taxes. When the Whiskey Rebellion broke out in defiance to whiskey taxes, Meredith Clymer, George's son, was among the military force that put down the insurrection. In a stroke of incredibly bad luck young Clymer was one of the few militiamen killed by the rebels. The elder Clymer was devastated and resigned his post. His last public service was at the end of Washington's second term in 1796 when the first president named Clymer to a panel that negotiated peace with the Creek and Cherokee nations in Georgia. A treaty was completed by the next year.

Through his remaining years, Clymer focused on philanthropic pursuits, raising funds for the University of Pennsylvania and serving as the president of the Pennsylvania Academy of Fine Arts. He served as president of the Philadelphia Society for Promoting Agriculture from 1805 to 1813. He was also president of the Philadelphia Bank from 1803 until his death.

George Clymer died at his son Henry's home in Morrisville, Pennsylvania, just across the Delaware River from Trenton, New Jersey, on January 23, 1813. He was 73 years old. None of the obituaries mentioned his signing of our nation's most important documents. He was laid to rest at the Friends' Burying Ground in Trenton, New Jersey, despite not being the place where he was born, lived, served, or died. He has a very simple grave that borders a parking lot.

The very modest grave of George Clymer at Friends Burying Ground in Trenton, New Jersey (photo by Lawrence Knorr).

Stephen Crane
(1709 – 1780)

"Bayoneted by Hessians"

Buried at First Presbyterian Church,
Elizabeth, New Jersey.

———•◦•———

Continental Association

Stephen Crane was a New Jersey sheriff, judge, and politician who was also a member of the First Continental Congress, where he signed the Continental Association. Crane worked for many years to unite East and West New Jersey into one state. He was wantonly killed by Hessian soldiers on their way to battle in 1780. While his contributions to the American Revolution are mostly forgotten, many of his descendants were noteworthy, including his namesake, a great-great-grandson who wrote *The Red Badge of Courage*.

———◆◦◆———

Crane, born circa 1709 in Elizabethtown, New Jersey, was one of five sons of Daniel Crane and his wife, Hannah Susannah (née Miller) Crane. He married Phoebe, maiden name lost to history, and the couple had seven children.

In 1743, the town elders selected Crane to travel to England with Matthias Hatfield to present a petition to King George II regarding colonial matters, likely about the festering divisions between East and West New Jersey. Several years later, he was elected to the town committee in 1750. He also served as the high sheriff and a judge of the Court of

Stephen Crane

Common Pleas. From 1766 to 1773, Crane was a member of the New Jersey General Assembly, including a stint as speaker in 1771.

Next, Crane was elected the mayor of Elizabethtown. As hostilities increased with England, Crane served on the New Jersey Committee of Correspondence and Inquiry in 1774 and 1775. In June 1774, he was president of the convention that nominated delegates to the Continental Congress. He himself was nominated, and from 1774 to 1776, Crane was elected to the Continental Congress, where he signed the Continental Association.

Following his wife's passing, he declined to continue in Congress and remained in New Jersey to deal with the East/West divisions. He continued to serve in the New Jersey legislature and other local positions. In the meantime, Elizabethtown was at the center of Hessian and British troop movements to and from Staten Island. In 1779, Crane's ferry building, a parsonage, and other structures were burned by Hessians led by Baron von Knyphausen.

On June 23, 1780, while on their way to the Battle of Springfield, Hessian soldiers passing through Elizabethtown bayonetted Crane, mortally wounding him. According to a bronze marker erected in 1913 by the Daughters of the American Revolution:

> Here the British turned into Galloping Hill Road from Elizabethtown to Connecticut Farms and Springfield at the time of the battles June 7 and 23, 1780. Washington afterwards said of the New Jersey militia "They flew to arms universally, and acted with a spirit equal to anything I have seen during the war." A son of Gen. William Crane is said to have been bayoneted to death by British soldiers near this spot.

Author Stephen Crane, the great-great-grandson of the patriot.

Why was Crane, a seventy-year-old man bayonetted by soldiers? Crane was not in the military, but he was known to have been one of the organizers of the rebellion. Perhaps Crane was taunting the troops, angry at the burning of his ferry building the prior year. It should be noted Crane was the grandfather of General William Crane and not the son.

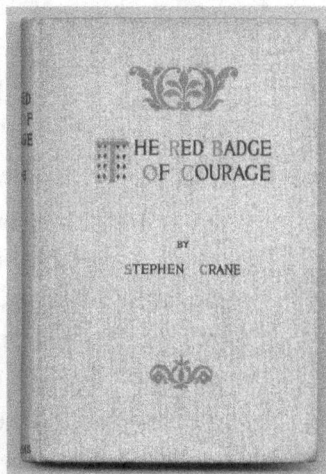

Stephen Crane died from his bayonet wounds on July 1 and was buried at the First Presbyterian Church in Elizabeth

Crane's famous novel.

next to his wife and father. His gravestone reads, "Sacred to the Memory of Stephen Cane Esq. who departed this Life July Year A.D. 1780 In the 71 Year of his Age."

He was the only civilian member of the Continental Congress killed by the enemy.

Among Crane's many descendants:

- Grandson William Crane (1778–1830) served as mayor of Essex County, New Jersey, and fought in the War of 1812 with Richard Montgomery at the Battle of Quebec, eventually losing a leg from his injuries. He rose to brigadier general of the New Jersey militia following the war.
- Grandson Ichabod Crane (1787–1857) served in the US Marine Corps and fought in the War of 1812, rising to the rank of colonel. He served aboard the USS *United States*.
- Grandson Joseph Halsey Crane (1782–1851) served as an Anti-Jacksonian member of the US House of Representatives from Ohio (1829–37).
- Great-grandson Charles Henry Crane (1825–1883) was a brigadier general and served as Surgeon General of the United States (1882–83).
- Great-grandson Jonathan Townley Crane (1819–1880), author and clergyman who was the father of author Stephen Crane.
- Great-great-grandson and namesake Stephen Crane (1871–1900) became famous through his numerous written works, including *Maggie: A Girl of the Streets* (1883), and *The Red Badge of Courage* (1895). He died at age 28 from tuberculosis.
- Painter Bruce Crane (1857–1937).

The grave of Stephen Crane.

Jonathan Dayton
(1760 – 1824)

Youngest Constitution Signer

Buried at St. John's Episcopal Church,
Elizabeth, New Jersey.

———•◆•———

United States Constitution

Jonathan Dayton was a leading American political figure who represented New Jersey through most of his political career. He was the youngest person to sign the U. S. Constitution and a member of the U.S. House of Representatives, serving as its fourth Speaker and later in the U.S. Senate. His political career waned after he was arrested in 1807 for alleged treason in connection with Aaron Burr. He was subsequently exonerated by a grand jury.

———◆◆◆———

Dayton was born in Elizabethtown (now Elizabeth), New Jersey, to his father, Elias Dayton, who was a storekeeper and was active in local politics, and his mother, Hannah (née Rolfe) Dayton, on October 16, 1760. Elias served as a militia officer in the French and Indian War, and the family was prominent in the community. Elizabethtown had a good reputation for education because of a local academy led by a famous educator, Tapping Reeve, and his protégé, Francis Barber. Two of Dayton's schoolmates at the academy were Alexander Hamilton and Aaron Burr. He then went on to attend the College of New Jersey (today's Princeton University).

Jonathan Dayton

In late 1774, the First Continental Congress called for a boycott of goods imported from England, and both Daytons allied themselves with the Revolutionary Movement and served on Elizabethtown's enforcement committee. When the war broke out in 1775, Dayton quit college and joined the Continental Army, serving under his father in the 3rd New Jersey Regiment. He was fifteen. Despite missing his final year at Princeton, he still graduated with his class and was later awarded an honorary Doctor of Laws degree.

On January 1, 1777, Dayton was commissioned a lieutenant. He soon found himself engaged in heavy skirmishing with British forces threatening Philadelphia, the American capital. When the British tried a flank attack by sea, Dayton's 3rd New Jersey accompanied Washington in a march to Pennsylvania and saw action in battles at Brandywine Creek and Germantown. He remained with Washington at Valley Forge and received solid training under Frederick von Steuben.

In October 1780, Dayton and his uncle, Lieutenant Colonel Matthias Ogden, were captured by a Loyalist raiding party. They spent the winter as prisoners in New York and were then released. Dayton returned to New Jersey, was promoted to captain and sent to Yorktown, where he fought in the decisive battle. During the siege, he led his company in the crucial nighttime bayonet attack on Redoubt 10 under the command of his old schoolmate, Alexander Hamilton. When the war ended, Dayton remained in the service until the Army was dissolved in 1783.

After the war, Dayton turned to studying law and taking part in the family's merchant business. He opened a law practice and divided his time between land speculation, law, and politics. He was a member of the New Jersey General Assembly in 1786 and 1787. In 1787, his father, Elias, was offered to represent New Jersey at the Constitutional Convention in Philadelphia. He declined in favor of his son. At the convention, he spoke with moderate frequency, and although objecting to some provisions of the Constitution, he signed it. He was the youngest person to sign it at 26 years old.

After the Constitutional Convention, Dayton enjoyed a good reputation in his home state. He was elected to the First Congress but preferred instead to become a member of the New Jersey Council and Speaker of the State Assembly. In 1791, he was again elected to the U.S. House of Representatives, but this time he took office and served four consecutive terms. During the last two terms, he served as Speaker of the House (1796–1799).

Beginning in 1799, he served a single term in the U.S. Senate, part of the moderate segment of the Federalist Party. He was pragmatic in his approach and, for example, crossed party lines to support President Jefferson's purchase of the Louisiana Territory.

Dayton had become wealthy mainly due to his heavy investment in land speculation in the Ohio region. He owned nearly a quarter million acres. The city of Dayton, Ohio, was named after Jonathan Dayton in 1796. His wealth made him attractive to his old classmate, Aaron Burr, who approached Dayton for financial assistance with plans he had for lands west of the Appalachian Mountains. There are multiple theories as to what Burr's plans were. In *The Burr Conspiracy* by James E. Lewis

Jr., the author notes that Burr enticed others to join him with plans to liberate Spanish Mexico, with promises of western lands, or with a plan to create a new western empire. President Jefferson, who didn't trust Burr, embraced the latter theory. His administration ordered the arrest of Burr and others, including Dayton. Burr was charged with treason, but the evidence against him was thin and confusing, and he was acquitted. Dayton's case went to a grand jury, where he was exonerated. Although the charges were never proven, his political career was finished on the national level. Except for a one-year term in the New Jersey legislature, he retired from public life.

Shortly before his death on October 9, 1824, Dayton entertained his old comrade-in-arms, Lafayette, in Elizabethtown on his grand tour of the United States. He was interred in an unmarked grave that is reportedly now under the St. John's Episcopal Church in Elizabeth, New Jersey, which replaced an original church in 1860. Our attempts to visit his grave were unsuccessful, as the place seemed abandoned. Our calls went unanswered, and our messages were unreturned. It seems a shame that he is so under-memorialized after contributing so much.

Dayton's grave lost in the weeds in Elizabeth, New Jersey.

John DeHart
(1727 – 1795)

Mayor of Elizabethtown

Buried at St. John's Episcopal Churchyard,
Elizabeth, New Jersey.

Continental Association

John DeHart was a delegate from New Jersey to the Continental Congresses in 1774 and 1775. He was one of the signers of the Continental Association and a member of the committee that prepared the draft for the New Jersey State Constitution in June 1776. He was elected Chief Justice of the State Supreme Court in 1776 and later elected Mayor of Elizabethtown in 1789.

John DeHart was born in Elizabethtown (now Elizabeth) in Union County, New Jersey, on July 25, 1727. His parents were Jacob and Abigail DeHart. He was one of four children, having a brother and two sisters. His brother, Captain Jacob DeHart, was in the British military and died in Haiti in 1758—perhaps during the Seven Years War.

He completed preparatory studies and then took up the study of law. In 1756, he married Sarah Dagworthy. Record keeping being imprecise in those days it is uncertain how many children the couple had. Various sources have them with three, eight, and twelve. DeHart was admitted to the New Jersey Colonial Bar in 1770 and opened a law practice.

On July 21, 1774, he was named as a delegate to the first Continental Congress along with James Kinsey, William Livingston, Stephen Crane, and Robert Smith. The Congress opened on September 5, 1774. DeHart

John DeHart

was in favor of reconciliation with Britain, although he supported the first Petition to the King and the non-importation agreement. The Petition to the King was a letter to King George III in October by Congress calling for the repeal of the Intolerable Acts. It contained a statement of loyalty to the Crown and became known as the Olive Branch Petition. The King rejected the Petition, although he never gave a formal reply. The non-importation agreement was part of the Continental Association, which DeHart signed along with 53 of the 56 members of the first Congress.

In 1775, DeHart was returned to the Second Continental Congress. As differences with Great Britain became more pronounced, Congress took a harder line, and DeHart became more alienated from his peers. Finally, on November 13, 1775, he wrote his resignation to the New Jersey Assembly. The Assembly accepted it on November 22. The following June 22, 1776, New Jersey appointed an entirely new delegation to the Continental Congress and authorized them to vote for independence. They were Abraham Clark, John Hart (not to be confused with John DeHart), Francis Hopkinson, Richard Stockton, and John Witherspoon.

After his service in the Continental Congress ended, DeHart came home to New Jersey and helped prepare the draft bill that eventually became the New Jersey State Constitution when enacted in June 1776. Later that year, he was appointed as Chief Justice of the new New Jersey Supreme Court but also practiced law. Governor William Livingston replaced him in February 1777 for failing to attend court sessions.

While the status of his children are uncertain, DeHart had three nephews who fought in the Revolution—sons of his brother Dr. Mattias DeHart.

In 1789, he was elected as the Mayor of Elizabethtown and served until his death. He died at his home in Elizabeth on June 1, 1795, at the age of 67. He is buried in St. John's Episcopal Churchyard in Elizabeth. On our attempt to visit his grave and the burial place of a more prominent founder, Jonathan Dayton, who is also buried there, we found an overgrown, neglected, inaccessible cemetery. Attempts to reach anyone there were unsuccessful. Numerous subsequent phone messages went unanswered.

The grave of John DeHart.

John Hart
(1713–1779)

Washington Camped Here

Buried at Hopewell Baptist Meeting House Cemetery,
Hopewell, New Jersey.

Declaration of Independence

John Hart was a public official in colonial New Jersey who, although he received very little formal schooling, developed a reputation for honesty and generosity that led him to be selected as a delegate to the Second Continental Congress and a signer of the Declaration of Independence.

Sources disagree as to the year and place of Hart's birth but most biographers have put it in 1713, in Hopewell, New Jersey. He was named for his grandfather who was a carpenter from Long Island. John's father Edward was a farmer, Justice of the Peace, and leader of a local militia unit during the French and Indian War. Edward moved to Hopewell at about the age of 20, married Martha Furman in 1712, and they had five children.

John was baptized at the Maidenhead Meetinghouse (now the Presbyterian Church of Lawrenceville) on December 31, 1713. He learned to read and write and do math but received very little formal education. He was a poor speller but was well known for his common sense and considered knowledgeable about money and business matters. He was attracted to a young lady named Deborah Scudder and rode thirty miles round trip to see her. They married in 1739 and had 13 children.

Portrait of John Hart, artist unknown.

In 1740, he started to acquire land and soon was the largest landowner in Hopewell. In 1747, he donated a piece of his land to local Baptists who had been seeking a place to build a church. John was a Presbyterian and thus his donation endeared him to the Baptists in the area.

John Hart began his public service in 1750 when he was elected to the Hunterdon County Board of Chosen Freeholders, the highest elected office in the county. In 1755, he was elected Justice of the Peace and was thereafter called John Hart, Esquire.

In 1761, he was elected to the Provincial Assembly of New Jersey. There he pressed for New Jersey to participate in the Stamp Act Congress, in New York in 1765. He was particularly disgusted with the Stamp Act. The tax was trifling but it involved a principle. It gave the Crown power over the colonies against the arbitrary exercise of which they had no protection. This meant that they had little control over their own property. It might be taxed in the manner and to the extent which Parliament pleased, and not a single voice represented the colonies.

He would serve in that assembly until 1771. In 1768, he was appointed as a judge to the Court of Common Pleas. He was often called "Honest John." In 1775, he was elected to the Committee of Correspondence of New Jersey which was a vehicle for the colonies to keep each other informed about developments regarding the Revolution.

In 1776, New Jersey formed a revolutionary assembly and Hart was elected and served as vice president. The New Jersey delegation to the First Continental Congress was opposed to independence. On June 22, 1776, he was elected as one of five New Jersey delegates to the Second Continental Congress with authorization to vote for independence. His fellow delegates were Abraham Clark, Francis

The fine grave of John Hart at Hopewell Baptist Meeting House Cemetery in Hopewell, New Jersey (photo by Lawrence Knorr).

Hopkinson, Richard Stockton, and John Witherspoon. Hart voted for the Declaration of Independence and was the thirteenth to sign it. He and the others were now branded traitors by King George III.

He served in Congress until August and then was elected to the New Jersey State Assembly where days later he was elected its speaker. On October 5, he returned home to attend to his sick wife. On October 8, 1776, Deborah Hart died.

On November 13, the British invaded the state and in December advanced into Hunterdon County. A marked man due to his status as Speaker of the Assembly, Hart had to hide from the British and the Hessians who were hunting for him, at one point hiding in a natural rock formation called the Rock House. The Hessians ravaged the Hopewell area and Hart's home and property suffered severe damage. Two of his

Detail from John Hart's monument (photo by Lawrence Knorr).

young children took refuge in the homes of relatives. Great effort was made to capture him and fellow New Jersey signer Richard Stockton. Though Hart was able to elude the British, Stockton was not and was held under deplorable conditions. The Continentals capture of Trenton on December 26 allowed Hart to return home. He collected his family and went to work repairing his home and farm. He was re-elected twice as Speaker of the Assembly and served until November 1778.

In June 1778, Hart invited the American army to camp at his farm. Washington accepted his invitation and 12,000 men occupied his fields from June 22 to June 24 and at least once General Washington dined with their host. Two days after leaving, the troops fought the British at the Battle of Monmouth.

On November 7, 1778, Hart returned from the Assembly in Trenton. Two days later, he was too sick with "gravel" (kidney stones) to return. He continued to suffer a slow and painful death until he succumbed on May 11, 1779, at the age of 66.

John Hart and his wife were laid to rest at the Hopewell Baptist Meeting House Cemetery on the same ground that Hart had donated for the building of the Baptist church. His grave is marked by a beautiful obelisk and bronze plaque. The date on the obelisk for his death is

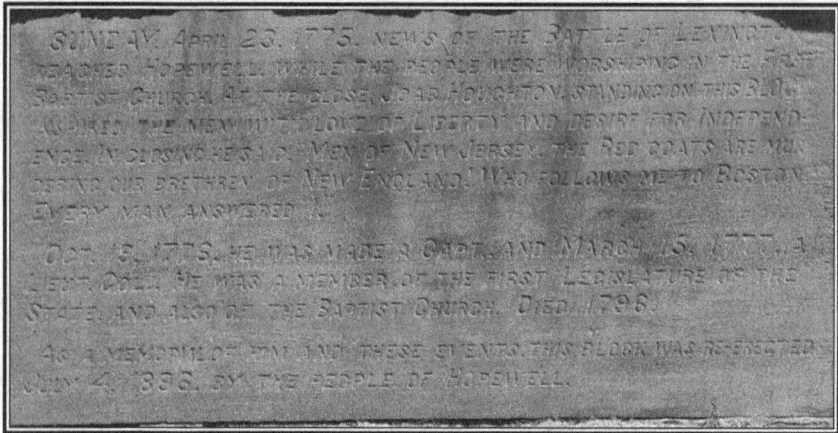

Detail of the monument honoring Joab Houghton at Hopewell Baptist Meeting House Cemetery (photo by Lawrence Knorr).

1780 but most biographers and the *New Jersey Gazette* say he died on May 11, 1779.

Next to Hart's grave is the grave of Joab Houghton. A memorial to him was erected by the people of Hopewell and dedicated in 1896. On the face of the memorial is inscribed "Sunday, April 23, 1775, news of the Battle of Lexington reached Hopewell when the people were worshiping in the First Baptist Church. At the close, Joab Houghton, standing on this stone, inspired the men with love of liberty and desire for independence. In closing, he said, "Men of New Jersey, the Red Coats are murdering your brethren in New England! Who follows me to Boston?" Every man said "Aye". Houghton went on to serve as a lieutenant colonel in the Revolutionary Army.

Francis Hopkinson
(1737 – 1791)

The Patriot Renaissance Man

Buried at Christ Church Burial Ground,
Philadelphia, Pennsylvania.

Declaration of Independence

In 1924 a Pennsylvanian historian wrote that this founder was a poet and a scientist. As it turns out, that description is an understatement. He was also a mathematician, mechanic, musician, composer, inventor of musical instruments, a lawyer by profession, and a signer of the Declaration of Independence. He was a man who could indeed be termed a Jack of many arts and perhaps a master of some. His name was Francis Hopkinson.

Hopkinson was born in Philadelphia on September 21, 1737. His father, Thomas Hopkinson, was a close friend of Benjamin Franklin. The duo was so close that they co-founded the University of Pennsylvania. It is not surprising that Hopkinson himself was a member of the first class educated by the college his father helped establish. He graduated in 1757 and received a master's degree in 1760.

After college Hopkinson studied law under Benjamin Chew, who was the Attorney General of the province. He was admitted to the bar in 1761 and was considered an able lawyer. However, his many interests encroached on both his ability and time to practice law. In the same year, he was admitted to the bar he was called upon to perform his initial act of public service. He served as secretary to a conference held on the banks of the Lehigh

Francis Hopkinson

River between the Indians of that area and Governor James Hamilton. He wrote a poem titled "The Treaty" that was inspired by this experience.

In 1766 he sailed for Europe where he lived for approximately a year in Ireland and England. When he returned to America, he resumed his law practice and opened a dry goods business in Philadelphia. In 1768 he married a Jersey girl, Ann Borden, and the couple would produce five children including the jurist and statesman Joseph Hopkinson who wrote the lyrics to "Hail Columbia." That song was recognized by many as the de facto national anthem of the United States until the country adopted "The Star-Spangled Banner" when that piece was recognized as the official anthem by Congress in 1931.

After his marriage, Hopkinson moved to Bordentown, New Jersey. When he first entered the practice of law, Hopkinson took legal positions supporting the crown. However, as time passed, he grew to favor American independence, and he resigned from the English colonial government positions. In June of 1776, he was elected to represent New Jersey in the

Second Continental Congress. As a member of Congress, he made enough of an impression on John Adams that the future president conveyed his thoughts on Hopkinson in a letter to his wife, Abigail. Adams wrote, "I met Mr. Francis Hopkinson, late a mandamus councilor of New Jersey, now a member of Continental Congress, who was liberally educated and is now a painter and a poet. I have a curiosity to delve a little deeper into the bosom of this curious gentleman, and may possibly give you more particulars concerning him. He is one of your pretty, little, curious, ingenious men. His head is no bigger than a large apple. I have not met with anything in natural history more amusing and entertaining than his personal appearance, yet he is genteel and well-bred and very social." There is little doubt that Adams was pleased when Hopkinson voted in favor of independence and subsequently signed the document declaring the same.

As a member of Congress, Hopkinson served as the Treasurer of Loans in the young nation's Treasury Department. He also wrote patriotic songs and drew caricatures of other members of Congress. One of the songs he composed titled "The Battle of the Kegs" became the best known of all ballads written during the Revolutionary period. He also worked on designing seals for various agencies of the government and was a member of the committee given the job of designing the Great Seal of the United States.

In 1779 Hopkinson was appointed to the position of Judge of the Admiralty for Pennsylvania. He served in this position until 1789. In that same year, President Washington made him the United States District Judge for Pennsylvania; a position he would hold until his death.

Hopkinson also used his talents to support the ratification of the Constitution. In 1787 he wrote the poem and allegorical essay "The New Roof" to aid in the effort to have the states accept the new form of government that the Constitutional Convention had proposed. In the work, he describes architects who had discovered a weakness in a mansion house composed of thirteen rafters in need of repair. The rafters represented the original colonies. His work ends with the words, "Figure to yourselves, my good fellows, a man with a cow and a horse—oh the battlements, the battlements, they will fall upon his cow, they will fall upon his horse and wound them, and the poor man will perish with hunger. The architects of the new structure (Constitution) would save both the building and the man's possessions."

In 1927 Dr. G. E. Hastings, a professor of English at the University of Arkansas, asserted that Hopkinson and not Betsy Ross was the actual designer of the first American flag. Hastings based his claim on his examination of documents in the archives of the Congressional Library. There he found that Hopkinson had submitted a bill to Congress that requested payment for the work he had done designing the flag. His asking price was "a Quarter cask of the Public Wine." Congress responded by saying that as an employee of the Treasury, his pay had covered any work he had done. While he was never paid, Hastings and other historians have correctly concluded that Hopkinson is the only person in the minutes of the Continental Congress credited with having designed a United States flag.

According to Doctor Benjamin Rush, Hopkinson was "seized with an apoplectic fit" on the morning of May 9, 1791. He died shortly after that and was laid to rest in Philadelphia's Christ Church Burial Ground. As a result of rumors that he wasn't buried in that cemetery, remains were exhumed in the 1930s and inspected by a University of Pennsylvania anatomist. The conclusion was that the remains were Hopkinson's. As his tombstone had deteriorated over the years, when he was reburied, a new memorial was added to the site. Among the credits now listed on the bronze plaque that rests above him is "Designer of the American Flag."

The grave of Francis Hopkinson.

James Kinsey
(1731–1802)

The Jurist from Jersey

Buried at Friends Burying Ground,
Burlington, New Jersey

———◆•◆———

Continental Congress • Continental Association

This founder was born in Pennsylvania, but he made a name for himself in neighboring New Jersey. A lawyer, after being admitted to the bar he practiced his craft in both of the aforementioned states. He served as a member of the New Jersey General Assembly. He represented that state as a member of the Continental Congress from July 23, 1774, until November 22, 1775. In Congress, he was one of the signers of the Continental Association. In 1789, he was appointed chief justice of the New Jersey Supreme Court, and he served in that position until he died in 1802. His name was James Kinsey.

———◆•◆———

Kinsey was born in Philadelphia on March 22, 1731. His father, John Kinsey, was a prominent Philadelphia attorney. In 1919, James Issac Sharpless wrote, "After William Penn, no colonial Quaker had the absolute confidence of Friends in church affairs, and at the same time the strong leadership in the state to the extent possessed by John Kinsey. During the last decade of his life, he was the clerk of the yearly meeting and its most responsible and influential member. He was also the chief justice of the Supreme Court of the Province, Speaker of the Assembly and the undoubted leader of its party in political management.

James Kinsey

Kinsey's Education was centered in Philadelphia local schools. He then studied law and was admitted to the New Jersey colonial bar in 1753. While he practiced law in both Pennsylvania and New Jersey, he resided in Burlington County which was located in the latter named colony. He began his political career in 1772 when he was elected to the Colonial General Assembly. He also served as a member of the Committee of Correspondence for Burlington County.

In July of 1774, the New Jersey General Assembly elected Kinsey to represent the colony at a meeting set to convene that September in Philadelphia, a gathering that became known as the First Continental Congress. That Congress brought together representatives of 12 of the 13 colonies. The meeting was brought about by the British decision to blockade Boston Harbor and Parliament's passage of the Intolerable Acts as a response to the Boston Tea Party. The Congress agreed on a Declaration of Resolves that included the Continental Association. Kinsey added his signature to the Continental Association.

The Association, which was passed on October 20, 1774, is considered to be a major accomplishment of the initial Congress. It called for a trade boycott against British merchants. Congress believed that economic sanctions on British imports and exports would pressure Parliament to deal with colonial grievances and the repeal of the very unpopular Intolerable Acts.

The General Assemblies of each colony, with the exception of New York, approved the de+idioms made by the Congress. The boycott was implemented, but any hope that it would be successful in changing British behavior ended with the outbreak of hostilities in April of 1775.

Prior to adjourning, the First Congress voted to meet again the following year if their grievances had not been addressed. This gathering became the Second Continental Congress, and this time every colony sent representatives. Once again, Kinsey was among the New Jersey delegates. The Second Congress convened in Philadelphia on May 10, 1775. Kinsey, a Quaker, opposed war and was not in favor of independence. Perhaps because he saw the direction the Congress was heading with regard to independence, Kinsey resigned in November of 1775. His resignation was accepted.

Kinsey's is among the many unmarked graves at the Burlington Friends Cemetery.

Returning to New Jersey, Kinsey served on the state's Supreme Court until his death in January 1802. After his death, *The New York Evening Post* printed the following:

> The valuable and eminent qualities of this worthy gentleman are too well and generally known to us and in need of an obituary eulogium, independence of mind, ever disdaining to stoop even in the appearance of dissimulation; manly rectitude of principle and unspoiled integrity, directing a vigorous and enlightened under-standing; honorable and social pursuits were the strongly marked textures of his public character.

Kinsey was laid to rest in the Friends Burying Ground located in Burlington, New Jersey.

Nathaniel Scudder
(1733–1781)

"The Only Congressman to Die in Battle"

Buried at Old Tennent Churchyard,
Tennent, New Jersey.

———•◆•———

Articles of Confederation • Military

Nathaniel Scudder was a physician and Continental Congressman who signed the Articles of Confederation. He was also an officer in the New Jersey Militia during the American Revolution and was killed in action. Scudder was the only former member of the Continental Congress killed in battle.

———◆◆◆———

Scudder, born May 10, 1733, in Monmouth Court House, New Jersey, was the son of Jacob Scudder and his wife, Abia (née Rowe) Scudder.

Scudder was a 1751 graduate of the College of New Jersey (now Princeton University). He studied medicine and then opened a practice in Monmouth County. He married Isabella Anderson with whom he had five children. He was also, as of December 1766, one of the board members of Mattisonia Grammar School in Lower Freehold, New Jersey, along with Reverand William Tennent and Reverand Charles M. Knight.

In 1774, as hostilities increased with England, Scudder joined the county's Committee of Safety and was elected to attend the Provincial Congress of New Jersey. By 1776, Scudder was elevated to the New

Portrait of Nathaniel Scudder.

Jersey Committee of Safety and became the Speaker of the New Jersey Assembly. He also joined the New Jersey Militia as a lieutenant colonel.

On November 20, 1777, Scudder was elected to the Continental Congress which met in York, Pennsylvania. He was re-elected the following year, serving with Abraham Clark, Elias Boudinot, Jonathan Elmer, and John Witherspoon back in Philadelphia.

The summer of 1778 was especially busy for Scudder, who had abandoned his medical practice and was splitting his time between Congress and the New Jersey Militia. On June 28, 1778, he led his regiment at the Battle of Monmouth, very close to his birthplace. He also wrote a series of impassioned letters about the progress of the Articles of Confederation. In a letter to John Hart on July 13, 1778, he worried about the delay in the ratification of the Articles of Confederation:

> I do myself the Honor to address you upon an Affair to me one
> of the most serious and alarming Importance. The Honorable

Council and Assembly of this State have not thought proper to invest their Delegates with Power to ratify and sign the [Articles of] Confederation; and it is obvious that unless every [one] of the thirteen States shall accede to it, we remain an unconfederated [sic] People. These States have actually entered into a Treaty with the Court of Versailles as a Confederated People and Monsieur Girard their ambassador Plenipotentiary to Congress is now on our Coast with a powerfull [sic] Fleet of Ships, which have taken Pilots on Board for Delaware. He probably may be landed by this Time, and will at all Events be in Philadelphia in a few Days. How must he be astonished & confounded? [A]nd what may be the fatal Consequences to America, when he discovers (which he will immediately do) that we are ipso facto unconfederated [sic], and consequently, what our Enemies have called us, 'a Rope of Sand'? Will he not have just Cause to resent the Deception? [A]nd may not insidious Britain, knowing the same, take Advantage of our Disunion? For my own Part I am of Opinion She will never desist from her nefarious Designs, nor ever consider her Attempts upon our Liberties fruitless and vain, untill [sic] she knows the golden knot is actually tied. I left Congress last Wednesday Evening. The Affair of Confederation was to be taken up next Day. The Magna Charta of America was amply engrossed and prepared for signing. Ten States had actually authorised [sic] their Delegates to ratify; a Delegate from an eleventh (vizt. Georgia) declared he was so fully possessed of the Sense of his Constituents, that he should not hesitate to subscribe it.

New Jersey ratified the Articles of Confederation on November 19, 1778. John Witherspoon signed with Nathaniel Scudder. Scudder was elected to the Continental Congress again in 1779.

Finished in the Continental Congress, Scudder next served in the New Jersey General Assembly in 1780. He also continued his military service and was promoted to colonel in 1781. On October 17, 1781, he led part of his regiment to counter a foraging party from the British Army near Shrewsbury, New Jersey and was killed in the skirmish at Blacks Point. He was buried at the Tennent Church Graveyard in

Tennent, Monmouth County, New Jersey, three days later, the same day the British surrendered at Yorktown.

Scudder was the only member of the Continental Congress to die in battle. He was also the last colonel to die in battle during the American Revolution.

Scudder's tombstone reads, "In Memory of the Honorable Nathaniel Scudder, Who Fell in Defence of His Country October the 16th 1781 Aged 48 Years."

The grave of Nathaniel Scudder.

Richard Smith
(1735 – 1803)

Congressional Diarist

Buried at Unknown,
Natchez, Mississippi.

Continental Association

Richard Smith was a signer of the Continental Association during his service in the Continental Congress from 1774–1776 as a delegate from New Jersey. An attorney by trade, he is best known for his detailed diary kept regarding the proceedings. Smith was also briefly the Treasurer of New Jersey in 1776.

Born on March 22, 1735, Richard was the son of Richard "The Elder" and Abigail (nee Raper) Smith who resided in Burlington, New Jersey. The family were Quakers, descended from William Smith of Bramham Parish, West Riding, Yorkshire County in the 1500s. Richard "The Elder" was the first child of Samuel and Elizabeth Smith. He was born in Burlington, New Jersey on July 5, 1699, and died at Perth Amboy on November 9, 1751. He was a successful merchant who built and owned vessels involved in the sugar trade with the West Indies. The Smith sons would often accompany him on voyages.

Young Richard attended schools run by the Society of Friends, also known as the Quakers, as well as private tutors provided by his wealthy parents. He studied law under Joseph Galloway and was accepted into the Pennsylvania colonial bar in Philadelphia. He practiced law there for

Portrait of Richard Smith etched from a silhouette,
artist unknown.

a while before returning to Burlington. In 1762 he married Elizabeth
Rodman, with whom he had five children. On December 7, 1762, he
was named the county clerk of Burlington County.

In 1768, following the Treaty of Fort Stanwix with the Iroquois
Confederacy, 69,000 acres between the Susquehanna and Mohawk
Rivers were ceded to New York. This is in what is now Otsego County.
Smith and other speculators received large portions of this land. He decided to visit the tract with Robert Wells and others, keeping a detailed
journal of the trip, including observations about the geography, econom-
ics, flora, fauna, and people of the area comprising the valleys of the
Hudson, Mohawk, Susquehanna, and Delaware rivers. This journal was
later published in 1906 as *A Tour of Four Great Rivers*. Smith returned
to the area many times and, in 1773, he built a house called "Smith

Hall" on 4,000 acres on both sides of the Otsdawa Creek in what is now Laurens, New York.

While Richard followed a course of colonial and state offices, his brother Samuel followed in the father's footsteps as a successful merchant. Samuel did become the treasurer of the Western Division of New Jersey and, in 1763, became a justice of the peace and then a member of the New Jersey Council. Later, he became the Treasurer of New Jersey. Samuel died suddenly in Burlington on July 13, 1776, while serving in this capacity at the age of 55. Richard returned to New Jersey to replace him in that role.

The New Jersey Committee of Safety elected Richard Smith as a delegate to the First Continental Congress on July 23, 1774. He was reelected on January 24, 1775, and February 14, 1776. He attended sessions from September 5, 1774 to October 26, 1774, May 10, 1775 to August 2, 1775 (except for his attendance of the New Jersey Assembly as clerk from May 15 to 20, 1775), September 12 to 30, 1775, and December 13, 1775, to March 30, 1776.

Smith kept a detailed diary of the events during these critical times, recording the events of September 1775 to March 1776. Along with the diaries of John Adams and Samuel Ward, it is one of the few personal records of these proceedings and provides insights not officially recorded. As an example, on 12 September 1775, Smith wrote:

> I attended at Congress for the first Time since the Adjornment [sic]. Mr. [John] Hancock having a Touch of the Gout there was no President in the Chair. The Colonies of New Hampshire and N Carolina absent as also sundry Members from other Colonies. Dr. [Benjamin] Franklin read several Letters recieved [sic] today by Capt. Falkner from London and informed the Members that he had some Bales of Household Goods on Board of Falkner, desiring the Congress's Leave to land them. [N]o Objection to it only [Thomas] Willing [of Pennsylvania] and John Rutledge thought it irregular to do Business without a President and it was referred. Mr. Gadsden and others moved for an Adjornment [sic] to 10 Tomorrow, which was complyed [sic] with. 3 of the Georgia

Delegates were present with Mr. Peyton Randolph and the new Delegates from Virginia, their Credentials not yet delivered, and little Business hitherto done this session.

It appears Smith spent a great deal of time listening and writing rather than speaking. There are few mentions of him in the proceedings except to say he was one of the delegates from New Jersey. Smith was from a conservative, mostly Loyalist section of his state. He signed the

This church is near the original city cemetery in Natchez, Mississippi where Richard Smith is likely buried in an unmarked grave (photo by Lawrence Knorr).

Continental Association on December 1, 1774, putting in place economic sanctions against Great Britain. The following year, he did affix his
name to the Olive Branch Petition on July 5, 1775, its aim to avoid war.

During his involvement with the New Jersey Provincial Congress in
January 1776, he penned a letter to Lord Stirling, one of Washington's
subordinates, regarding the treatment of prisoners of war, including 1000
dollars from the Continental Treasury to fund them.

A month before the Declaration of Independence, citing poor health
(of his brother), Richard resigned his position with the Continental
Congress and returned to New Jersey. John Hart took his place in the
Congress and signed the Declaration. Following his brother's death,
Smith focused on New Jersey, holding the position of Treasurer until he
resigned on February 15, 1777. He returned to practicing law. In 1790,
he moved his family to Laurens, Otsego County, New York, but returned
to Philadelphia after less than ten years. His son, Richard R. Smith, was
the first sheriff in the new Otsego County.

Around this time, he had developed a lingering illness. Upon the
advice of his physician, Smith went on a trip to the South to improve his
health. Unfortunately, while in Natchez, Mississippi on September 17,
1803, he passed away at the age of 68. For many years, there have been
advertisements seeking information about the burial location of Richard
Smith. While some believe he is interred in the Natchez City Cemetery,
this institution did not exist until 1822. It is likely Smith was buried else-
where and then possibly moved in 1822 with a number of other graves.
If so, his grave remains unmarked.

"Smith Hall" was afterward known as "Otsego Hall" and was the
early home of Fenimore Cooper, whose father had been an agent for the
Smiths and had acquired the property from them.

Richard Stockton
(1730 – 1781)

A Most Ingenious Fellow

Buried at Stony Brook Quaker Meeting House Burial Grounds,
Princeton, New Jersey.

Declaration of Independence

This Founder was born into wealth and after graduating from the College of New Jersey in 1748 became a well known New Jersey lawyer. He was also treated well by the English crown who appointed him to the Royal Supreme Court of New Jersey. In his spare time, he collected works of art and bred horses. He recognized that as the troubles between England and the colonies grew he could lose everything, including his life if he opposed the crown. In 1776 he willingly joined other patriots in supporting American independence. New Jersey chose him to be one of their delegates to the Second Continental Congress. It was in this capacity that he affixed his signature to the Declaration of Independence. This action cost him his wealth and his health. It is no exaggeration to say that no signer suffered more for his autograph than Richard Stockton.

Stockton was born on October 1, 1730, near Princeton, New Jersey. His father, John Stockton, was a wealthy landowner who donated property to what is now Princeton University. After graduating college, Stockton studied law under David Ogden in Newark. In 1754 he was admitted to the bar and in 1763 he was made a sergeant of the law

Portrait of Richard Stockton by John Wollaston.

which was the highest degree in the field of law attainable at the time. During this period, he married the poet Annis Boudinot Stockton and the couple produced six children.

Stockton was not your run of the mill revolutionary. His wife was an accomplished poet and the couple resided in his father's mansion located in Princeton. He loved both art and horses and spent much of his free time collecting the former and raising the latter. However, it appears that Stockton was impressed by the arguments made by those who favored a break with Britain. In time his views changed from Americans ruling themselves but pledging allegiance to King George to a total separation from the mother country. On July 2, 1776, as a member of the Continental Congress, Stockton voted yea on the question of independence. He was the first representative from New Jersey to sign the document Jefferson authored.

In the fall of 1776 Stockton and fellow signer George Clymer were sent to upstate New York to inspect the troops. The two were appalled at the lack of supplies, in particular the lack of adequate clothing for the troops. After hearing that the British army was approaching Princeton, Stockton returned to his home where, rather than gather his family and taking flight, he stayed and helped feed and clothe the American soldiers in the area. When those soldiers retreated, Stockton gathered his family and traveled to a home of a friend about thirty miles away in Monmouth County. A loyalist recognized Stockton and alerted others loyal to the British of his presence. He was roused from his sleep, taken prisoner, turned over to the English army, and eventually sent to Provost Prison in New York where he was starved and subjected to brutally freezing temperatures. Meanwhile, his estate in Princeton was occupied by General Cornwallis. All his household belongings and livestock were seized and his library burned. Anything that the British couldn't carry with them they destroyed.

When word reached Congress that Stockton was in prison and in failing health, a resolution was passed instructing General Washington to attempt to gain his release. While Washington did attempt to negotiate a prisoner exchange, it appears that Stockton was released only after signing a loyalty pledge in which he agreed to cease any war efforts against England.

Stockton's time in prison did not kill him but it robbed him of his health. In a letter written in March of 1777, fellow Declaration signer John Witherspoon reported that Stockton was back home but was sick from "cold and exhaustion." Within a few years, he was stricken with cancer and underwent a painful operation to have a growth removed from his lip. The cancer eventually spread to his throat and he passed away at the age of 50 on February 28, 1781. He was laid to rest in the Stony Brook Quaker Meeting House Cemetery Grounds in Princeton, New Jersey.

There are those who view Stockton as the only signer to recant the Declaration in order to gain his freedom. It is important to remember that after his release he again declared his loyalty to the United States. George Washington never harbored any ill feelings towards Stockton whom he considered a friend. After the signer from New Jersey passed away, Washington wrote his widow saying that she could rest assured that "we can never forget our friend . . ." Washington wished all Americans should never forget the sacrifices made and the hardships suffered by Richard Stockton in his service to his country.

Marker for Richard Stockton at Stony Brook Quaker Meeting House Burial Ground in Princeton, New Jersey (photo by Lawrence Knorr).

John Witherspoon
(1723 – 1794)

President of Princeton

Buried at Princeton Cemetery,
Princeton, New Jersey.

———•–•–•———

Declaration of Independence • Articles of Confederation

John Witherspoon is a hard man to understand. He was a renowned theologian from Scotland who was invited to be president of the College of New Jersey, now Princeton University. He was extraordinarily successful in that role and went on to embrace the revolutionary cause. He was the only clergyman to sign the Declaration of Independence and the Articles of Confederation. He also served at the convention that ratified the U.S. Constitution in New Jersey. He was a highly active member of the Continental Congress and served in the New Jersey state government. Yet Witherspoon owned slaves and lectured *against* the abolition of slavery.

———⇒•⇐———

He was born in Gifford, Scotland, and received the finest education available at that time. He attended the preparatory school in Haddington, Scotland, and obtained a master of arts degree from the University of Edinburgh in 1739. He remained at Edinburgh to study divinity. In 1764 he was awarded an honorary doctoral degree in divinity by the University of St. Andrews. In 1743 he became a Presbyterian Minister at a parish in Beith, Scotland, where he married Elizabeth Montgomery. The

John Witherspoon

couple had ten children, with five surviving to adulthood. He remained in Beith until 1758 and, in that time, authored three notable works on theology. From 1758 to 1768, he was minister of the Laigh Kirk, Paisley, a large growing parish church. There he became very prominent within the church.

Witherspoon was aggressively recruited by the trustees of the College of New Jersey in 1766, who needed a first-rate scholar to serve as its president. He was at first unable to accept due to his wife's great fear of crossing the sea. The trustees persisted, particularly Richard Stockton and Benjamin Rush, who visited the Witherspoons and convinced them to accept. He had a comfortable life and was well respected in the U.K., so it was a big decision. They arrived in Philadelphia in early August of 1768.

He enjoyed great success at the college. He turned it into a remarkably successful institution and was extremely popular as a result. He wrote frequent essays on subjects of interest to the colonies. He taught courses and recruited quality staff and students. Moral Philosophy was a required course as he considered it vital for ministers, lawyers, and those in government. Among his students were five delegates to the U.S. Constitutional Convention, including James Madison. Among his students came 37 judges (3 became Supreme Court Justices), 10 Cabinet officers, 12 members of the Continental Congress, 28 U.S. Senators, and 49 Congressmen.

While Witherspoon first abstained from political concerns, he came to support the revolution, joining the Committee of Correspondence and Safety in early 1774. The British referred to his college as a "seminary of sedition." He was passionate about American independence and the necessity of checks and balances for an ethical form of government. Following along the traditions of John Locke, he believed that "because of the depravity of human nature, government power needs to be carefully limited and separated among branches and levels . . . to prevent any one level, any one branch, or any one individual in government from becoming too powerful."

In 1776 he was elected to the Continental Congress, where he voted for Richard Henry Lee's famous resolution for independence and the Declaration of Independence. He was one of the most active members of the Congress, serving on an exceptionally large number (Over 120) of committees, was appointed Congressional Chaplain, helped draft the Articles of Confederation, helped organize the executive departments, and drew up the instructions for the Peace Commissioners. Perhaps his most important contribution during the war happened due to his role on the Committee for Foreign Affairs. Fluent in French, he wrote a letter to a French agent introducing Ben Franklin and explaining the necessity of an alliance between the colonies and France, without which the course of the revolutionists might have been lost.

The year 1777 was tough for John Witherspoon. His son Major James Witherspoon was killed at the Battle of Germantown, and as the fighting neared Princeton, he closed and evacuated the college. The main

Witherspoon bronze at Princteon.

building, Nassau Hall, was severely damaged, and his papers were lost. The school remained closed for several years.

Witherspoon left the Continental Congress in November 1782 to rebuild his beloved Princeton. During the summer of 1783, the Continental Congress met in Nassau Hall, making Princeton the nation's capital for four months. Between 1783 and 1789, he sat for two terms in the New Jersey Legislature and strongly supported the adoption of the Constitution during the ratification debates. In 1789 his wife Elizabeth died. In 1791 the 68-year-old delighted the college community by marrying a 24-year-old widow, Ann Dill, with whom he had two daughters.

Witherspoon's last years were filled with difficulty. He lost one eye on a fundraising trip to Great Britain in 1784 and lost his sight completely in 1792. On November 15, 1794, he died at his farm at the age of 71 and was buried along President's Row in Princeton Cemetery.

An inventory of Witherspoon's possessions taken at his death included two slaves valued at $100 each. This deeply religious man, who required all his students to attend his lectures on moral philosophy, owned slaves and lectured against the abolition of slavery. In 1779 when he moved from the President's House on campus to the newly completed country home called "Tusculum" he purchased two slaves to help him run the 500-acre estate. When helping to draft the Articles of Confederation, Witherspoon sided with Southern states and adamantly opposed the taxation of slaves, comparing slaves to horses as simply another form of

The grave of John Witherspoon.

property. In 1782 he gave lectures disapproving of the slave trade, yet he owned slaves and retained ownership of them.

For all his discussion about the injustice of holding men in bondage "by no better right than superior power," he ultimately concluded that emancipating them was not necessary, stating, "I do not think there lies any necessity on those who found men in a state of slavery, to make them free to their own ruin."

This conclusion conveniently absolved him and other slaveholders of their moral dilemma. Slavery continued in New Jersey until the end of the Civil War.

Sources

Books, Magazines, Journals, Files:

Alexander, Edward P. *Revolutionary Conservative: James Duane of New York*. New York: Ams Press, 1978.

Anthony, Katharine Susan. *First Lady of the Revolution; The Life of Mercy Otis Warren*. Port Washington, N.Y.: Kennikat Press, 1972.

Appleby, Joyce. *Inheriting the Revolution: The First Generation of Americans*. Cambridge, Massachusetts: Harvard University Press, 2000.

Atkinson, Rick. *The British Are Coming: The War for America, Lexington to Princeton, 1775-1777*. New York: Henry Holt & Co. 2019.

Bordewich, Fergus M. *The First Congress: How James Madison, George Washington, and a Group of Extraordinary Men Invented the Government*. New York: Simon and Schuster Paperbacks, 2016.

Boudreau, George W. *Independence: A Guide to Historic Philadelphia*. Yardley, Pennsylvania: Westholme Publishing, LLC. 2012.

Bowen, Catherine Drinker. *Miracle at Philadelphia: The Story of the Constitutional Convention May to September 1787*. Boston, Massachusetts: Little, Brown & Company, 1966.

Breen, T.H, *George Washington's Journey: The President Forges a New Nation*. New York: Simon & Schuster. 2016.

Brookhiser, Richard. *Gentleman Revolutionary: Gouverneur Morris The Rake Who Wrote the Constitution*. New York: Free Press, 2003.

———. *John Marshall: The Man Who Made the Supreme Court*. New York: Basic Books. 2018.

Brush, Edward Hale. *Rufus King and His Times*. New York: N.L. Brown, 1926.

Chadwick, Bruce. I Am Murdered: *George Wythe, Thomas Jefferson, and the Killing That Shocked a New Nation*. Hoboken, New Jersey: John Wiley & Sons, 2009.

Chambers, II, John Whiteclay. *The Oxford Companion to American Military History*. Oxford: Oxford University Press, 1999.

Commager, Henry Steele & Richard B. Morris. *The Spirit of 'Seventy-Six: The Story of the American Revolution as Told by Participants*. New York: Harper & Rowe, 1967.

Cole, Ryan. *Light-Horse Harry Lee: The Rise and Fall of a Revolutionary Hero*. Washington, D.C.: Regnery History. 2019.

Conlin, Joseph R. *The Morrow Book of Quotations in American History*. New York: William Morrow and Company, Inc., 1984.

Daniels, Jonathan. *Ordeal of Ambition*. Garden City, New York: Doubleday & Company, Inc., 1970.

Dann, John C. *The Revolution Remembered: Eyewitness Accounts of the War for Independence*. Chicago: University of Chicago Press, 1980.

SOURCES

DeRose, Chris. *Founding Rivals: Madison vs. Monroe: The Bill of Rights and the Election that Saved a Nation.* New York: MJF Books, 2011.

Drury, Bob & Tom Clavin. *Valley Forge.* New York: Simon & Schuster. 2018.

Ellis, Joseph J. *Revolutionary Summer: The Birth of American Independence.* New York: Alfred A. Knopf, 2013.

———. *The Quartet: Orchestrating the Second American Revolution, 1783-1789.* New York: Alfred A. Knopf, 2015.

———. *His Excellency: George Washington.* New York: Alfred A. Knopf, 2004.

Flexner, James Thomas. *George Washington in the American Revolution, 1775-1783.* Boston: Little, Brown & Company, 1967.

Flower, Lenore Embick. "Visit of President George Washington to Carlisle, 1794." Carlisle, Pennsylvania: The Hamilton Library and Cumberland County Historical Society, 1932.

Gerlach, Don R. *Proud Patriot: Philip Schuyler and the War of Independence, 1775-1783.* Syracuse, N.Y.: Syracuse University Press, 1987.

Goodrich, Charles A. *Lives of the Signers of the Declaration of Independence.* Charlotteville, N.Y.: SamHar Press, 1976.

Griffith, IV, William R. *The Battle of Lake George: England's First Triumph in the French and Indian War.* Charleston, South Carolina: The History Press, 2016.

Grossman, Mark. *Encyclopedia of the Continental Congress.* Armenia, New York: Grey House Publishing, 2015.

Hamilton, Edward P. *Fort Ticonderoga: Key to a Continent.* Boston: Little, Brown & Company, 1964.

Isenberg, Nancy. *Fallen Founder: The Life of Aaron Burr.* New York: Penguin Group, 2007.

Kennedy, Roger G. *Burr, Hamilton, and Jefferson: A Study in Character.* New York: Oxford University Press, 1999.

Kiernan, Denise & Joseph D'Agnese. *Signing Their Lives Away: The Fame and Misfortune of the Men Who Signed the Declaration of Independence.* Philadelphia: Quirk Books, 2008.

———. *Signing Their Rights Away: The Fame and Misfortune of the Men Who Signed the United States Constitution.* Philadelphia: Quirk Books, 2011.

Klarman, Michael J. *The Framers' Coup: The Making of the United States Constitution.* New York: Oxford University Press, 2016.

Langguth, A. J. *Patriots.* New York: Simon and Schuster, 1988.

Larson, Edward J. *A Magnificent Catastrophe.* New York: Free Press, 2007.

Lee, Mike. Written *Out of History: The Forgotten Founders Who Fought Big Government.* New York: Penguin Books, 2017.

Lewis, James E., Jr., *The Burr Conspiracy: Uncovering the Story of an Early American Crisis,* Princeton: Princeton University Press, 2017.

Lockridge, Ross Franklin. *The Harrisons.* 1941.

Lomask, Milton. *Aaron Burr: The Years from Princeton to Vice President, 1756-1805.* New York: Farrar Straus Giroux, 1979.

Lossing, Benson J. *Pictorial Field Book of the Revolution.* New York: Harper Brothers. 1851.

Maier, Pauline. *American Scripture: Making the Declaration of Independence*. New York: Alfred A. Knopf, Inc., 1997.

McCullough, David. *John Adams*. New York: Simon & Schuster, 2002.

Meltzer, Brad & Josh Mensch. *The First Conspiracy: The Secret Plot to Kill George Washington*. New York: Flat Iron Books. 2018.

Middlekauff, Robert. *The Glorious Cause: The American Revolution, 1763-1789*. Oxford: Oxford University Press, 2005.

Miller, Jr., Arthur P. & Marjorie L. Miller. *Pennsylvania Battlefields and Military Landmarks*. Mechanicsburg, Pennsylvania: Stackpole Books, 2000.

Millett, Allan R. & Peter Maslowski. *For the Common Defense: A Military History of the United States of America*. New York: The Free Press, 1984.

Moore, Charles. *The Family Life of George Washington*. New York: Houghton Mifflin, 1926.

Nagel, Paul C. *The Lees of Virginia: Seven Generations of an American Family*. Oxford: Oxford University Press, 1990.

O'Connell, Robert L. *Revolutionary: George Washington at War*. New York: Random House. 2019.

Racove, Jack N. *Revolutionaries: A New History of the Invention of America*. New York: Houghton Mifflin Harcourt, 2011.

Raphael, Ray. Founding Myths: *Stories That Hide Our Patriotic Past*. New York: MJF Books, 2004.

Rossiter, Clinton. *1787 The Grand Convention*. New York: The Macmillan Company, 1966.

Seymour, Joseph. *The Pennsylvania Associators, 1747-1777*. Yardley, Pennsylvania: Westholme Publishing, LLC. 2012.

Schweikart, Larry & Michael Allen. *A Patriot's History of the United States from Columbus's Great Discovery to the War on Terror*. New York: Penguin, 2004.

Sharp, Arthur G. *Not Your Father's Founders*. Avon, Massachusetts: Adams Media, 2012.

Stahr, Walter. *John Jay: Founding Father*. New York: Diversion Books, 2017.

Taafee, Stephen R. *The Philadelphia Campaign, 1777-1778*. Lawrence, Kansas: University of Kansas Press, 2003.

Tinkcom, Harry Marlin, *The Republicans and the Federalists in Pennsylvania, 1790-1801*. Harrisburg, Pennsylvania: Pennsylvania Historical and Museum Commission. 1950.

Ward, Matthew C. *Breaking the Backcountry: The Seven Years' War in Virginia and Pennsylvania, 1754-1765*. Pittsburgh, Pennsylvania: University of Pittsburgh Press, 2003.

Weisberger, Bernard A. *America Afire: Jefferson, Adams, and the Revolutionary Election of 1800*. New York: HarperCollins, 2000.

Wood, Gordon S. *The Radicalism of the American Revolution*. New York: Vintage Books, 1993.

———. *Empire of Liberty: A History of the Early Republic, 1789-1815*. New York: Penguin Books, 2004.

———. *Revolutionary Characters: What Made the Founders Different*. New York: Penguin Books, 2006.

SOURCES

————. *The Americanization of Benjamin Franklin*. Oxford: Oxford University Press, 2009.

Wright, Benjamin F. *The Federalist: The Famous Papers on the Principles of American Government: Alexander Hamilton, James Madison, John Jay*. New York: Metro Books, 2002.

Zobel, Hiller B. *The Boston Massacre*. New York: W. W. Norton & Company, 1970.

Video Resources:

Guelzo, Allen C. The Great Courses: *America's Founding Fathers* (Course N. 8525). Chantilly, Virginia: The Teaching Company, 2017.

Online Resources:

Archives.gov – for information on the Constitutional Convention.

CauseofLiberty.blogspot.com – for information on Daniel Carroll.

ColonialHall.com – for information about the signers of the Declaration of Independence.

DSDI1776.com – for information on many Founders.

FamousAmericans.net – for information on many Founders.

FindaGrave.com – for burial information, vital statistics and obituaries.

FirstLadies.org – for information on Abigail Adams.

Newspapers.com – Hundreds of newspaper articles were accessed—too numerous to mention here.

NPS.gov – for information on various park sites.

TeachingAmericanHistory.com – for information on Charles Pinckney and George Wythe.

TheHistoryJunkie.com – for information on multiple Founders.

USHistory.org – for information on multiple Founders.

Wikipedia.com – for general historical information.

Index

INDEX

www.ingramcontent.com/pod-product-compliance
Lightning Source LLC
LaVergne TN
LVHW030631080426
835512LV00021B/3449